A Teacher's Guide
To Engineer Learning

GRAND DESIGNS

Ellen Williams

Annette Brinkman

Gary Forlini

LAVENDER HILL PRESS
Bronxville, New York 10708

Art and Design: Rose marie James

Printed and bound in the U.S.A.

Library of Congress Cataloging-in-Publication Data

Grand Designs: A Teacher's Guide To Engineer Learning—first edition

LCCN No.: 2009911113

ISBN-13:   978-0-9796424-5-6
ISBN-10:   0-9796426-5-0

10 9 8 7 6 5 4 3 2 1

Published by: Lavender Hill Press
                  an imprint of Research in Media, Inc.
                  P.O. Box Ten
                  Bronxville, New York 10708

To contact Lavender Hill Press directly, call **914-725-7800** or write **info@lavenderhillpress.com**

Acknowledgements

We wish to thank the many teachers and administrators who daily bring their many insights and experiences into play to help and support fellow educators and, ultimately, to benefit students. Among those legions of devoted teachers and leaders, including many creative "planners" who helped inspire this book, we wish to give special thanks to these whose words and ideas directly benefited our own thinking, "planning," and developing of *Grand Designs*.

Tim Frost
Sue Savage
Matthew Shepherd
Paul Shepherd
Sheri Lyn Sohm

CONTENTS

In the beginning ...

Afterword. And the verdict is ...

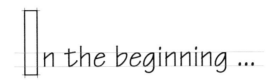

Principal Viola Lacey took a chance on a young mathematics teacher fresh out of grad school because she had been impressed by her new hire's answers to search committee questions, especially her ideas about differentiating her lessons to meet varying student needs and interests.

Viola had been impressed by Mary Pat's model lesson. Not only had she established clear expectations at the outset by posting a well-focused Learning Outcome, she also presented Success Criteria for students containing specific sub-skills. And most impressive to Viola was the way Mary Pat referenced those sub-skills during the lesson AND engaged individual students in self-assessing as their work progressed. "You planned that lesson very carefully, didn't you?" she asked Mary Pat on their first staff development day of the year. They sat in Viola's office before the day's meetings were scheduled to begin. With them was Clay Briggs, the mentor assigned to her.

"I did. I studied lesson design in school, and I knew what I wanted to accomplish with students. Also, your cooperating teacher gave me useful information in advance about the individuals in his class. There were such wide gaps in their abilities!"

"Mary Pat and I have been reviewing her students' learning profiles," Clay said, "and she's come to the same conclusion about her classes this year—wide variations in the abilities and even the cultures and languages of her students."

"I have work to do," Mary Pat added. "I know that, and I'm excited by the challenge."

"That's why I asked you two to meet with me this morning." Viola leaned forward in her chair. "This is very important to me and to all of us. A critical instructional goal that I've set with the faculty for this year is incorporating formative assessment into daily lessons. I've asked everybody to increase their focus on that level of lesson planning that includes specific tactics for assessing student progress in real time and for providing ways for students to self assess."

"I think Mary Pat has made a great start on that," Clay offered. "In my first visit to her class I saw the same attention to planning that you saw in her model lessons. She was working with two groups at the white board doing problem solving, and she had each student use colored cups to show progress. Red meant they got the answer wrong. Green was they got it right. Yellow meant 'I need more time!' It worked really well."

"It's a 'traffic signal technique' that I learned about," Mary Pat said. "I plan to hunt for even more ways that students can signal me about their status."

"That is a great start," Viola agreed. "Have the two of you identified specific areas—in addition to formative assessment, of course—that you will be working on?"

"We have," Clay said. "Mary Pat and I talked about using positive verbal cues to remind students about what they need to know and generally to engage them and hold their attention. That's a challenge because she has large classes."

"Yes, I started learning every student's name—all 140 of them—on the first day of classes, and it was a little overwhelming. I just fell into using cueing techniques because it forced me to use each of their names …"

"…in context, right," Clay completed her sentence. "Mary Pat found ways to include every student by name in her positive feed-back statements as they went through the lesson."

"I concentrated on learning their names as quickly as pos-sible, and cueing gave me a way to connect directly with each one."

"The feedback aspect interests me." Viola asked Mary Pat, "Do you think of feedback statements on your feet as you teach?"

"That's what I did at first, but Clay and I talked more about it."

"We saw real value in giving feedback," Clay said, "because Mary Pat's students responded so well to things she pointed out, like how well Julio sketched a tetrahedron in order to calculate area."

"He's a bit of an artist," Mary Pat said.

"He really liked hearing that, too!"

"And I plan to bring that up again with him because he can use that skill in other ways in the future."

"So Mary Pat and I decided that feedback statements deserve special planning."

"And I've been making feedback statements a careful part of my lesson planning."

"I can't tell you how happy I am to hear that," Viola looked from one to the other, "because feedback fits perfectly well into formative assessment. The two of you may have much to offer the rest of Mary Pat's department, or the whole faculty, as we get deeper into our goals for the year."

"Well," Mary Pat blushed, "I just want to get it right. I'm really new at this."

"You couldn't be off to a better start," Viola stood.

As they left their principal's office and walked down the hall together, Clay laughed. "We may be seeing the start of your reputa-tion taking shape."

"What do you mean by that?"

"I couldn't help notice the initials on your day planner. M.P."

Mary Pat's blank expression met Clay's grin. "It stands for my name."

"Indeed it does. Or it will. MASTER PLANNER!"

A star climbed into view above the horizon.

How To Use This Guide

 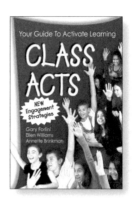

Grand Designs is about Planning for Effective Instruction

Class Acts is about Maximizing Student Engagement

Grand Designs focuses on different aspects of designing effective instruction. You may choose to read these chapters in sequence, especially if you are new to the profession. Or you might find these chapters most useful in a sequence that follows your planning needs as they develop.

Good planning requires attention to detail—so much detail that formulating really good instructional designs can feel overwhelming. For this reason, many of the chapters in *Grand Designs* give you examples and models of planning so that you can see how others have designed their instructional plans. At the very least, you can scan the plans that hold ideas for you, but always keep your thinking open to re-designing these plans to fit your needs, your curriculum, your students.

Class Acts, a companion book for *Grand Designs*, focuses on student engagement and classroom management. If you already have read *Class Acts*, think of it as a prequel to the deep dive of instructional design because it offers you techniques and experiences of teachers as they teach. On the other hand, if you are reading *Grand Designs* first, think of *Class Acts* as a sequel that can help guide your plans as you implement them. Either way, *Grand Designs* and *Class Acts* work hand-in-hand to inform most aspects of your professional practice.

What To Know about the Sources of This Information

Because *Grand Designs* derives from the knowledge and research of many leaders in education, every chapter ends with an invitation to "Consult Experts" where you will find a list of resources relating to the topics covered. Superscript references to many of those resources appear throughout each chapter to help connect you to additional readings should you wish to take an even deeper dive.

Grand Designs and *Class Acts* may offer you valuable support, especially if you work in a school or district that closely follows research-based standards, or frameworks, of teacher practice. For instance, your school or district may follow the framework of a recognized education leader like Charlotte Danielson (*The Danielson Framework for Teaching*) or Robert Marzano (*The Marzano Focused Teacher Evaluation Model*), or it may follow a state's specific framework like the *Utah Effective Teaching Standards* or that of a teacher-development organization like ObserverTab's TEAM framework (*Teacher Evaluation and Assistance Model*).

The information contained within these companion books *(Class Acts* and *Grand Designs)* correlate directly to the kinds of teacher-practice indications of the richest frameworks.

*Community planners understand the life styles
and needs of those who live and work there.*

Illustration: © Errol Hugh (modified)

Know Your Constituencies

students ... families ... cultures ... colleagues

Mary Pat Griffen had frequently heard—and she fully under-stood—the saying "It takes a village to raise a child," and with her mentor's help, she looked closely at the different worlds around her students—and the people who dwell there. She completed a self-assessment about Cultural Responsiveness (see page 23) which helped her focus on her strengths and needs. She shared it with Clay, her mentor, and then asked him and others in the school's guidance areas for information about her new students' support systems (parents, guardians, friends, other teachers).

Recognize the Variety of Cultures among Your Students

Your students possess significant knowledge about their fam-ilies, their communities, cultures, and related experiences. The more diverse your classroom, the more you have available to you in terms of values, cultural attributes, and unique experiences.

Get to know your students by listening to them and learning from them. Ask students and their families questions about their culture. Take the time to build a relationship with each student and family. Show your personal interest in their beliefs, language, customs, rituals, interests, etc. "Research demonstrates that schools benefit from families' funds of knowledge." [11]

Mary Pat set about doing just that even before she met her sixth graders on her official first day of teaching. She began with student records to identify the various cultural backgrounds that she could explore further. Specifically, she wanted to move beyond such obvious things as Asian cuisine and South American flags. *I won't ignore these kinds of things, of course,* she said to herself, but her mind raced ahead to opportunities for class discussions and fresh ideas that students might share which would lead to even more opportunities for students to work together—things like myths, fairy tales, oral and cultural histories, and literature.

Focus on Aspects of Each Culture in Your Classroom

To be a culturally responsive teacher, Mary Pat understood, she must explore each of those cultures not only to enrich her own knowledge of them, but also to enrich the environment of her classroom and the personal breadth of each student.

For sure, you must use the knowledge you have gained to respond to various cultural and individual needs of students. A student may have behavioral, dietary, or wardrobe characteristics that require attention in one way or another. On another level, however, all of those qualities and attributes hold promise for enhanced learning.

Specifically, you can enrich your curriculum and instruction by being culturally responsive. You might (1) use interdisciplinary strategies that connect student cultures in a cross-curricular manner, (2) incorporate students' real life experiences into lessons and activities, and (3) capitalize on students' cultural richness in classroom displays and other performance opportunities. [5]

To achieve any of these goals in your classroom, you must develop your ability to recognize the variety and depth of your students' cultural attributes.

Family Social Structures.

On a continuum of interdependence to independence, families differ. An interdependent family may have an extended family in which several family members plan guiding roles in your student's life, whereas an independent family may have one significant adult in the family. Knowing a student's family social structure, among other factors, will impact how you involve the family. For instance, in communicating with families of some students, you will need to extend beyond involving only one or both parents to a number of responsible adults. And for some students' families, you must be knowledgeable of other cultural circumstances before you plan family involvement activities.

Language of the Home.

The varying languages spoken in the home bring valuable knowledge to your lesson planning and the need for translation for family communication. For instance, speech patterns and language from student homes can differ from customary academic language of the classroom. Knowing key words from the language of the home can help you prepare to translate school information, thus improving your communication with families.

Interactional Behaviors and Styles.

Cultures differ in how they communicate with others, both verbally and nonverbally, which can impact one student's social behavior differently from another's. A student of one culture may exhibit a preference for directness while another, from a different culture, may value an indirect method of communication. Accordingly, a direct communicator may say precisely what s/he is thinking, whereas an indirect communicator may say less or only what s/he thinks you want to hear. Non-verbal behaviors may vary as well. For example, eye contact in some cultures is a sign of attentiveness while in other cultures, it is considered rude. Make every effort to recognize these interactional behaviors and styles in order to communicate sensitively and effectively with students and family members.

Educational Expectations.

Cultures differ in their perceptions regarding roles of family in the educational process. For example, some families may feel unwelcome inside the school, or they may not want to be intrusive, while others are more likely to feel the school will welcome their help in improving it. Be sensitive to these perceptions and begin opening up the conversation to encourage family involvement.

Acceptable Behaviors.

Be alert to unacceptable behavior in the context of a student's cultural background. Why? Acceptability varies across cultures; what is acceptable to one is unacceptable to another. For example, talking loudly or talking while others are talking may be entirely acceptable at home. Your responsibility is to show sensitivity when interacting with students and family members regarding your perception of unacceptable behavior. This does not mean that you accept the behavior; it means that you are coming from an understanding frame of mind when you explain and teach about appropriate behavior at school.

Inter-Cultural Variations.

Be careful not to paint any culture with broad brushstrokes. Cultural styles and attributes often vary within a culture. Keep in mind that not every person shares precisely the same beliefs, rituals, or behaviors. Take special care to avoid stereotyping students and families based on their cultures.

After the first few weeks of school, Mary Pat decided to take the self-assessment (p. 23) once more. It had been more than a month since she took it the first time, and during those weeks she began taking specific steps to know and engage her students. Her library research had yielded a wealth of stories from her students' cultures, and she was becoming adept at tailoring her instructional content as well as the physical environment of her classroom.

Taking the self-assessment once more allowed her to compare her ratings with her earlier assessment, which led her to conclude that she still had work to do. Her own ratings told her that she needs to focus on her interactions with families.

Develop a Collaborative System with Families

Think of your students' families not as clients but as partners in an educational community. Instead of doing things *for* them, think of doing things *with* them. Develop relationships with your students' families that are mutually engaging, collaborative.

So how do you do that?

Create a Welcoming Classroom Climate. Make personal contacts with families through email, phone calls, or home visits. Personally welcome family members into the classroom. Capitalize on family engagement activities to bring members into your learning community.

Communicate and Build Trusting Relationships. Make an initial and continuous positive contact with family. Open lines of communication through varying modes (technology, notes, phone calls, home visits, translators). Build trust by showing an interest in each family and keep your commitments. Be culturally sensitive in all communication.

Provide Actionable Information. Let family members know how they can support their child's learning. Connect families to workshops and materials on child development and the benefits of a family-school partnership. Send home a weekly or monthly suggestion on how to support learners at home.

Communicate along a Two-Way Street. Establish effective and positive school-to-home and home-to-school communication. Create a two-way communication method with each family. Use language of encouragement, cooperation, and support when communicating with families.

Engage, Engage, Engage. Engage families in classroom planning, leadership, and meaningful volunteer opportunities. Create significant roles for family members to assist in the classroom and in making important decisions for students. Create an open door policy, where families feel as if they are part of the learning community.

Create Community Connections. Connect students and families to community resources that strengthen and support students' learning and well-being. Create partnerships with community programs and connect families to the resources. Develop a service-learning project in which students and families interact and serve their local community.

Education experts such as Antunez[1] help us understand a wealth of research that has documented how increased family involvement in schools links to improved student performance regardless of socioeconomic status, ethnic/racial background, or parent education level. Make every effort to engage families into the learning community. Once your system of collaboration is established, you will begin to realize how family engagement is a significant key to student success.[2]

Work as Part of a High-Performing Team

In addition to working with her fellow colleagues and math teachers, Mary Pat was part of a grade-level/interdisciplinary team. In practice, she met formally twice a month with her department and each week with her team at a specified time. During the summer, she had formulated plans for working with families, but at the outset of the school year, she understood that working with colleagues on student learning requires attention to a very different set of circumstances and requirements.

Clay, her mentor, reminded her of this claim by experts on teacher collaboration:

> *Among the most powerful strategies for improving academic achievement for all learners is teachers meeting to collaborate around student learning.*[2]

Simply put, if teachers collaborate (e.g., in a pair, as a team, or as a department) to maximize student learning, they must also reach for best practices while communicating respect and regard for each other. So Mary Pat asked herself this vital question:

What does Effective Collaboration look like and sound like?

And Clay helped her recognize that a well-functioning team must shift its thinking from *I taught it*! to a laser-like focus on *Did students get it?*

Second, one must analyze approved curriculum standards to identify essential concepts and skills that every student must master. (See Chapter 3 for deeper information about unfolding a standard.)

Third, your team must design and administer pre- and post-common formative assessments that align with the articulated level of complexity of essential concepts and skills.

Fourth, you analyze and utilize data from common formative assessments to design differentiated first-time instruction and targeted intervention and enrichment for students.

And fifth, you engage in inquiry-based processes to hone your existing expertise while finding or developing new strategies that will best help students master essential learning. Keep this idea in mind:

Individual teachers on high-performing teams collaborate in good faith in ways that engender trust and regard.[3]

Like Mary Pat, if you work with colleagues on specific issues, discuss the importance of open communication among your team mates. Together, acknowledge that trust and regard lubricate the fine-grained decision-making conversations you engage in; with this idea in mind, you can reach your shared purpose of helping all students master essentials and grow beyond.

Tighten Team Functions

High-performing teacher teams move through developmental stages to learn and use effective practices that increase student learning. Even if your team has been working together for some time (and certainly if it is freshly minted), you must proceed through (or reflect upon) these 7 essential stages to ensure that you are at maximum power:

Stage 1: Use Your Time Productively

If you believe *Yes, we use our time together to make real progress*, then you have great potential as a team. However, if

you can honestly conclude that your team discussions are disjointed and rarely yield productive results, you must address this with frankness as well as a sense of shared renewal. Ask yourselves questions like *What distractions should we eliminate? What don't we yet understand fully? What don't students "get" that we must provide for?*

Stage 2: Share Personal Practice

Don't simply wonder what each of you does in your classrooms; talk about it. If this hasn't happened yet, start sharing personal classroom practices. Once you have a good idea about what each team member does (e.g., how each of you organizes for instruction), then you are well positioned for moving to the next developmental level, which is planning lessons together.

Stage 3: Plan, Plan, Plan

Each of you knows how to plan lessons. Maybe you design instruction by following approved curriculum standards or by constructing lessons around student textbooks. Each of you has a level of experience and expertise with planning. However, Effective Planning has two parts:

Instructional Planning *includes your expected outcomes, your materials, your methods and steps in instruction, etc. You are probably very good at plans like these.*

Assessment Planning *includes feedback from students as well as formative assessments built into your plans that will tell you whether students got it or already knew it before you taught it.*

Your team must work together collaboratively to craft both parts of the planning process in order to move from focusing on teaching *(I taught it!)* to ensuring that students actually learn *(Did they get it?)*.

Stage 4: Develop Common [Formative] Assessments

This stage is critical to ensuring that your teaching leads to student learning. Your team must ask questions:

> *At this grade level, what is essential for our*
> *students to know and be able to do?*
> *What does mastery look like and sound like?*
> *How will we know if students mastered essentials?* [2, 3]

Such questions will lead you toward developing common assessments to be administered to all students. Ultimately, the data from these pre- and post-common formative assessments give you useful road maps for subsequent planning and instruction. (Find more detail in Chapter Four.)

Stage 5: Analyze Student Learning

Once you have feedback from your formative assessments, you have information about each student's performance on each measured skill. Spend time with your team focusing on this data to articulate each student's status and needs—by concept and skill! This critical team time should yield a shared document—your roadmap—so that each of you will know precisely which students need support, which need enrichment, and which are on track to mastery.

Stage 6: Differentiate Your Follow-Up

At this point, you and your team utilize data from pre-common formative assessments. Look not only at the needs of each student, but also at patterns of performance among groups of students. For instance, you will see that certain students have mastered some skills but not others. Those students will need additional attention, perhaps even re-teaching of earlier, pre-requisite skills necessary to master new knowledge. Other students performed so well that they need enrichment right away. Or maybe far too many students do not "get" a particular concept, which suggests that you need to re-visit or re-teach your foundation lessons, possibly in a different way.

In short, the data patterns that you and your team identify will show you which concepts and skills require a short review and which need deep teaching. [2,4,6,7]

Stage 7: Reflect on Your Instruction

By noting the number of students who did or did not master each new concept or skill, you can tell which of your instructional practices succeeded and which need yet to be refined. Here's another way that your teamwork is essential: Use the data to spark instructional dialogue. Don't be afraid to ask which teachers' classrooms performed the highest on each concept or skill because your shared goal is to identify the most successful strategies to use with these particular students. (Hint: Next year's students may require an altogether different set of strategies; your data at that time will tell you so.) Your group reward is sharing knowledge of effective instructional practice. [6,7,12]

Consult Experts

1. Antunez, B.   "When Everyone Is Involved: Parents and Communities in School Reform." *Framing Effective Practice: Topics and Issues in the Education of English language learners.* Washington, DC: National Clearinghouse for Bilingual Education, 2000.

2. Bambrick-Santoya, P. *Driven by Data: A Practical Guide to Improve Instruction.* San Francisco, CA: John Wiley & Sons, Inc., 2010.

3. Bryk, A. and Schneider, B. "Trust in Schools: A Core Resource for School Reform." *Educational Leadership,* 2003.

4. Buffum, Mattos M. and Weber C. *Simplifying Response to Intervention: Four Essential Guiding Principles.* Bloomington, IN: Solution Tree Press, 2012.

5. Chartock, R. K. *Strategies and Lessons for Culturally Responsive Teaching: A Primer for K-12 Teachers.* Boston, MA: Pearson, 2010.

6. DuFour, R., DuFour, R. B., and Eaker, R. E. *Learning by Doing: A Handbook for Professional Learning Communities at Work.* Bloomington, IN: Solution Tree, 2006.

7. DuFour, R., DuFour, R. B., and Eaker, R. E. *Revisiting Professional Learning Communities at Work: New Insights for Improving Schools.* Bloomington, IN: Solution Tree, 2008.

8. Garmston, R.J. and Wellman, B.M., *The Adaptive School: A Sourcebook for Developing Collaborative Groups.* Norwood, MA: Christopher-Gordon Publishers, 1999.

9. Garmston, R.J. "Can Collaboration Be Taught?" *Journal of Staff Development* 18 (4), 1997.

10. Graham, P. and Ferriter, B.   "One Step at a Time." *Journal of Staff Development* 29 (3), 2008.

11. Moll, L.C., Amanti, C., Neff, D., and Gonzales, N. "Funds of Knowledge For Teaching: Using Qualitative Approach to Connect Homes and Classrooms." *Theory Into Practice* 31(2), 1992.

12. Schmoker, M.   *Results Now: How We Can Achieve Unprecedented Improvements in Teaching and Learning.* Alexandria, VA: Association for Supervision and Curriculum Development, 2006.

13. Voltz, D.L. and Morrow, S.H. "Enhancing Collaborative Partnerships With Culturally Diverse Families." *Classroom Leadership,* April, 1999.

Self Assess: Developing Cultural Responsiveness

For each element, self-assess using the following 1-4 scale:

1. **Missing (I need to do this)**
2. **Attempted (I try to do this, but I am not successful)**
3. **Apparent (I do this well, but I don't do it consistently. When I do it, it works!)**
4. **Well Done (I do this consistently and appropriately)**

Building Relationships with Students   1 2 3 4
I show a personal interest in my individual students'
beliefs, languages, customs, rituals, and interests.

Building Cultural Understanding   1 2 3 4
I learn and gather knowledge about the cultural attributes
of my students and their families.

Communicating Systematically with Families   1 2 3 4
I design and put into place positive, regular two-way
communication with each of my students' families and
invite family participation.

Communicating Responsively   1 2 3 4
I design my system of communication with home by
employing my knowledge of, and sensitivity to, the language
and cultural differences of each family.

Creating a Welcoming Classroom   1 2 3 4
I create a classroom climate that welcomes
students as well as their families.

Designing Culturally Responsive Lessons   1 2 3 4
I use the information I have gained through my students
and their families to design culturally responsive lessons
relating my lesson content to their cultural experiences.

Providing Actionable Information   1 2 3 4
I provide families with actionable information
to help them support their child's learning.

Creating Community Connections   1 2 3 4
I connect students and families with community resources.

Building Trusting Relationships with Families   1 2 3 4
I find concrete ways to build trusting, collaborative
relationships with all families so that together we can
promote student growth and development.

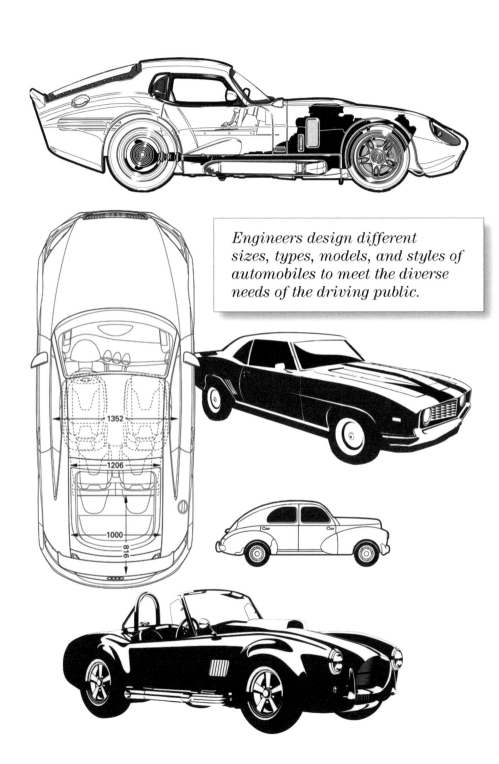

Engineers design different sizes, types, models, and styles of automobiles to meet the diverse needs of the driving public.

Keep Student Needs In Focus

styles ... profiles ... differentiation

By the second week of school, Mary Pat felt panic. Several of her students appeared disinterested while some others struggled with their problems—from the bell ringer set through the day's homework. She and her mentor Clay discussed the problem and identified students whom they thought needed alternative strategies. "Actually, I think Josh is bored," Clay suggested, "because he finishes before everyone else, and Maddie has trouble reading so she struggles to understand every word."

"I spent weeks mapping out my curriculum," Mary Pat said, "but I think what I've mapped out meets the needs of only about 50% of my students." The first step toward meeting these students' needs, she and Clay decided, was to look critically at their learning profiles—and that meant gathering additional information.

Focus Each Student's Strengths, Interests, and Needs

You can develop information about each student's learning profile by accessing information from existing school records and from colleagues. Add this information to your growing understanding of the qualities and needs of each, from their learning styles, personal interests, culture, and intellectual preferences to your formal and informal assessments and other individual variations. (Research offers you a wealth of information about this through the works of Gardner, Tomlinson, Turner and Hope, and others. See *Consult Experts*, p.42.)

A student's **learning profile** is comprised of many factors such as learning styles, gender, culture, intelligence preferences, and so forth.[1] Basic categories of learning styles, for instance, include auditory, kinesthetic, and visual learners. Auditory learners learn best by listening to verbal instruction or by engaging in verbal interaction with other students. Kinesthetic learners learn best by being physically active, manipulating concrete objects, dramatizing events, or engaging in other hands-on techniques. Visual learners capture information taking notes, by using color to highlight important ideas, reading, diagramming or sketching. These learners thrive when teachers illustrate ideas with diagrams or demonstrate concepts.[2,5]

While most students learn through a combination of learning styles, each tends to use a primary mode to obtain and make sense of information about the world. You can increase learning by understanding and using instructional strategies that provide opportunities for each student to learn through his or her preferred learning style.[2,3] For instance, Clay observed that Ellen excelled with hands-on activities but struggled with word problems so he suggested to Mary Pat that she devise alternative work with manipulatives for that student.

Keep in mind also that your learners also differ in their interests—those topics or areas of study for which they have an affinity or passion. When you provide opportunities for students to learn through their interests and to demonstrate their new knowledge and skills in multiple ways, you encourage them to be more highly motivated and to enjoy learning much more.

All of this information will help inform your awareness of each student's readiness for each entry point of learning. Some of your students may need pre-teaching or more opportunities for direct instruction, while others may have progressed beyond a particular entry point and may need extended content even before you begin the first teaching. And, surely, for many students, the designated grade level entry point for learning is just right.[1]

Be one of those teachers who actively seeks to learn, understand, and address each student's unique constellation of learning differences so that each can thrive academically and develop positive attitudes toward the process of learning.

Create Developmentally Appropriate Experiences

Don't think like this: *Every third grade student is taught the times tables the same month, whether they are ready for them or not, or whether they had already mastered them or not.* Or like this: *I have to make every eight grader practice recognizing sentence fragments—even my most accurate and gifted writers.*

Instead, follow this guiding premise: **Students differ in important ways.** And celebrate the uniqueness of each student while looking for qualities in each which open doors for fuller, richer learning. Take a deep look at the community inside your classroom. It likely is a mirror of your school's neighborhood, culturally and socially. You probably have students from various cultures and/or experiences, some learning a second language and a second culture. Some students are academically advanced and others are struggling with basic grade level standards. You have students with wide experiences and others who have limited opportunities. Now think about how you can ensure that every student learns as much and as quickly as possible. It may seem overwhelming, but it is doable!

How do you create developmentally appropriate and challenging learning experiences for the diverse needs in your classroom? For Mary Pat, that was her greatest question as the school year got underway. Clay put it this way: *"You're only going to feel like you're doing it right once you find and meet the unique needs of each one of your students."*

Research shows that teachers who design a differentiated classroom are well positioned to meet the needs of diverse students. Focus on designing a differentiated classroom, which means not teaching the class as though all students are alike. Respond to each learner's specific needs. Because students differ developmentally, academically, emotionally, and socially, you must find these differences and respond to individual student needs in specific and effective ways in order to maximize student success.

You can follow three guiding principles for differentiating your curriculum and instruction. Consider these:

1. **Develop a supportive and well-managed learning environment.** Recognize that it can sometimes, for some students, be counter-productive to provide the same amount of instruction, the same lessons, or the same learning materials for everyone. Instead, acknowledge each student's right to an education suited to his or her individual needs.

2. **Provide ongoing assessment to inform teaching and learning.** To be effective at differentiating, start with the knowledge of each student's aptitude, current skill level, and knowledge of the content. Begin the lesson with a pre-assessment to help you answer this question: *Who needs more background knowledge before I begin this lesson? Who already knows what I am about to teach? Who is just ready for this content?* Then as you deliver instruction, you must assess for student progress during the lesson as well as at the end to ensure students are learning the essential skills and concepts. The following diagram demonstrates an ongoing assessment loop:

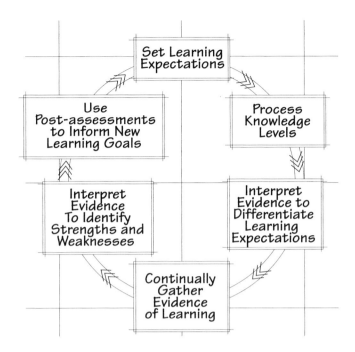

3. **Plan curriculum and instruction that responds to student differences.** Your pre-assessment gives you the data you need to tailor instruction accordingly, while your mid- and post-assessments keep you and them on track.

   Develop learning goals that vary according to the needs of individual students and by recognizing patterns in your data.

   Set pace, specifically time needed for the lesson(s) you have planned. For instance, advanced students may need more time on a complex lesson and less time on simpler ones. Conversely, struggling students may need a fast paced lesson to increase engagement or additional time on a complex assignment.

   Select materials that vary according to the needs of individuals or groups.

Choose modes of teaching to suit your understanding of student needs.   Choose from a wide variety of techniques (direct instruction, inquiry-based instruction, cooperative learning, problem-based learning, self-directed learning, and others) to deliver instruction that will work most effectively.

Use grouping as an organizational device for certain lessons or parts of lessons. Small groups, pairs, and independent learning all present themselves as possibilities for engaging students in concepts and skills. Use your judgement to determine which types of grouping will work best with which concepts and skills.

Consider flexible groups according to student interests, their skill levels, prior knowledge, previous performance, needs determined by your pre-assessment, and so forth. Because flexible grouping is a dynamic arrangement, you may want students to move from group to group according to the skills and activities that you plan for each. Such an approach can be powerful, but it requires careful planning—including designing pre-tests and mid-tests that guide your placement and movement of students—so that you ensure each student has a proper path through your design.

Assess, assess, assess because successful differentiated learning depends on it. Use a variety of assessments to evaluate background knowledge, skill level, interest level, ability, and learned outcomes as well as student progress during instruction.

Mary Pat knew that she needed help developing effective formative assessments, and since Viola, her principal, had made this a school-wide focus, her team was working on a variety of informal and formal types of assessments. In their first meetings, the team decided to identify methods that would not only assess student progress but also would be engaging for students. These are some of the methods they chose to assess pre-, mid-, and post-learning:

Informal Assessment Techniques	Formal Assessment Techniques
Written and Oral Reflections	Tests, Quizzes, Exams
Polls/Surveys	Teacher and Student Interview
Checks for Understanding	Online Learning Modules
Pair Shares	Projects, Presentations
Students Monitoring Their Own Learning	Portfolios

"Never lose sight of the power of personal interest," said science teacher Gil Kelton, a member of Mary Pat's interdisciplinary team. Indeed, researchers have found that student interest in a topic can enhance clarity in thinking, assist in deeper understanding, and can help students remember more accurately. Interest has the power to transform struggling performers and to lift high achievers to new planes.[4]

Look for Ways To Differentiate Curriculum and Instruction

Research focuses on three most effective ways to differentiate: (1) through Content knowledge and information, (2) through instructional Process, and (3) through student Product. Understand what each means:

CONTENT is information and ideas that students work with to reach learning goals. It is the essential knowledge, understandings, and skills of an area of study. You can differentiate content effectively by ...

- modifying how students access the content. Use pre- and post-assessment data to assist you in differentiating the material students are learning. As a simple example, if a student is directed to read something too simple or too complex, the student is less likely to learn.

- <u>modifying the pace at which the content is delivered.</u> Determine appropriate pace—slower or faster—depending on the complexity of the content and/or a need to engage students actively.

- <u>modifying the depth and complexity of the content.</u> To move students deeper into content, ask them to go from concrete to the abstract, from the familiar to the unfamiliar, and from the known to the unknown. To develop complexity in the content, incorporate issues, problems, and themes. Ask students to make relationships between and among ideas to connect diverse concepts and to explore content through interdisciplinary means.

PROCESS is the manner in which students make sense of content and develop skills. Emphasize higher-level thinking processes such as those outlined in models such as Bloom's Taxonomy, Paul's Reasoning Model, Creative Problem Solving, etc. (See Chapter 7 for more information about higher-order thinking and Chapter 8 for meta-cognitive skills.)

PRODUCT, or student product, are ways in which students demonstrate what they have learned and understood. It is how students show what they know, what they understand, and what they can do. Guide students to produce and present from their on-going learning in ways that are meaningful and that require manipulation of, or synthesis of, the content they are studying. Keep in mind that you want their product to demonstrate their understanding of the content.

Differentiate according to students' ...

- readiness (a student's proximity to specific learning goals).
- interests, passions, and other affinities that motivate learning.
- learning profile, which may include his or her preferred approaches to learning, intelligence preferences, gender, culture, etc.

When Viola visited Mary Pat's classroom, she observed differentiation in action. Later, when the two debriefed, Viola said, "You made it happen, girl. There was real differentiation at the heart of your instructional strategies. I saw you use a jigsaw activity for your students. I saw interest centers up and ready for them to further their study. And for Sue and Eliza, your top two students, I saw them working on deep independent study. I talked to them, and it was obvious to me that you had compacted their curriculum. You excused them from the material they had already mastered [Mary Pat made this decision from a pre-test] and gave them a research task that was taking them deeply into learning. Sue isn't always motivated or happy to be at school, but she was that day. I know this takes you a lot of extra planning time."

Differentiate through a range of instructional strategies by using...
• Compacting, Independent Study, Interest Centers, Interest Groups, Learning Centers, and Graphic Organizers.   • Questioning Strategies, Learning Contracts, Mentorships, Literature Circles, Jigsaw Activities, and Multiple Intelligences.   • Level Text, Supplemental Materials, Tiered Lessons, Journal Prompts.

As you plan for first-time instruction and as you assess and adjust your lessons along the way, keep in mind that your curriculum and instruction must respond effectively to student differences. Ensure that each student works in a supported and well-managed learning environment.

Creating the most productive learning experiences for your students must include communication between them and you—feedback (theirs), responsiveness (yours), and dynamic, continuing dialogue (all of you). Early stages of this work can include types of pre-assessment in which you elicit student feedback in a variety of ways, yet such interactions should continue during all stages of your work on a lesson, during a unit, and indeed for the length of your time with them.

See How Others Differentiate Their Lessons

Many teachers have success planning lessons that provide for individual learning needs and styles. Sharing lessons with colleagues is an excellent way to gain and build strategies. Here is just one example, a fifth grade teacher's plan to differentiate a lesson from the social studies curriculum. Careful planning to reach intended learning outcomes includes pathways for learners at a variety of levels.

In this plan, as a result of earlier formative assessments, this teacher has identified three pathways: one for students who are almost ready for the concept, one for students who are just now ready for the concept, and one for students who are ready to go beyond.

	A Differentiated Look at **Understanding the Causes and the Outcomes of the Boston Tea Party**
Universal Theme	*Change Can Be Evolutionary or Revolutionary*
Mode of Teaching	Inquiry and Cooperative Based Instruction
Background for Teacher	The teacher will need an understanding of the taxes imposed on the America Colonies, knowledge of the Boston Tea Party timeline, various protests about the taxes being imposed, the various political positions in1773, and the causes and outcomes of the Boston Tea Party.
Student Prior Knowledge	**Content:** Students understand taxation and self- government. **Process:** Students understand the process skill of cause and effect. **Product:** Students can write an essay and know the process of group discussion.
Intended Learning Outcomes	Students will understand how change can be evolutionary or revolutionary by investigating and analyzing the causes and effects of the Boston Tea Party.
Day One	Assess students on prior knowledge and interest level. Develop a spreadsheet of students' learning styles, prior knowledge level, and level of interests on this topic. Based on the pre-assessment outcomes place students into three groups: 1) Students who are almost ready for the concept, 2) Students who are just ready for the concept, and 3) Students who are ready to go beyond. These groups should be flexible as you assess and reassess for readiness throughout the unit.
Day Two	**Content:** Develop a deeper understanding of taxation and a lack of self-governing.

continued on next page

Day Two continued	**Students who are almost ready for the concept:**	• Each student is given a role: merchant, longshoreman, tea drinker, English Parli–amentarian, King, Patriot, and others. • Each student wears a sign that explains his or her role in the colony or in England and is given different amounts of currency depending on the role. • The King and English Parliamentarian announces to the group about the new taxes and decides how much they want to collect. • Taxes are collected. • Repeat bullets 3 and 4. • Group discussion and reflection about this process of being taxed without representation.
	Students who are just ready for the concept:	• In a small group, students discuss and record on a visual graphic the positive and negative elements of taxation. • Each student is given a role (listed above). In a mock town meeting they decide together how citizens can impact taxation. • Discuss and reflect on the positive and negatives of citizens' involvement in taxation.
	Students who are ready to go beyond:	• In a group, half of the group will take the role of lawmakers and the other half of the group will take the role of citizens. • Decide together what governmental services are important to keep and what services need to be discontinued to reduce taxes. Would you consider

continued on next page

Day Two continued		adding governmental services? Be sure to use research on what services are provided now. • As a committee, develop a rule for future taxation. Discuss the positive and negatives of representation on taxation.
Day Three and Four	**Content:** Students will investigate and research information. Each group will have an Investigator's Folder filled with information about different events leading up to and after the Boston Tea Party. Be sure to have materials in different forms of learning styles. Students research information on their topic.	
	Students who are almost ready for the concept:	Folder should contain: varying reading levels and address various learning styles (written, video, on-line activities). This group develops a timeline of events leading up to the Boston Tea Party.
	Students who are just ready for the concept:	Folder should contain: mostly on grade level and above reading level and various learning styles (written, video, on-line activities). This group develops a timeline of events during and after the Boston Tea Party.
	Students who are ready to go beyond:	Folder should contain: complex reading levels and learning styles (written, video, on-line activities). This group develops a visual graphic of the patterns and trends of the Boston Tea Party comparing it to a relatively current event that was also a change agent.

Plan for "Before," "During," and "After"

When you plan differentiation strategies for a lesson, be clear about the concepts and skills necessary for students to have already mastered (the "before"), be prepared to facilitate adjustments as learning takes place (the "during"), and take a reflective stance with students as you and they complete work (the "after").

Here are those three pointers again with examples from the 5th grade lesson on social studies.

Before, During, and After You Differentiate	
When?	How? (examples)
BEFORE: Be clear about concepts and skills necessary for students to have mastered before your lesson begins.	e.g., teach essay writing and group discussions. e.g., teach graphic organizers to show cause and effect.
DURING your lesson, prepare to facilitate adjustments.	e.g., plan to move certain students to different groups as a result of formal and informal assessments. e.g., set time limits, adjust pacing as necessary. e.g., analyze daily product to gauge student progress.
AFTER: Reflect with students.	e.g., hold a reflection group with students, ask students to share their graphics, group folders, etc.

Incorporate Tools of Language Development

Very few students come into your classroom as masters of their language, whether it be English or any other, and your English language learners (ELLs) may need intensive development with most or many aspects of English, which you can supply.

Your most reliable tools can be these simple few:

Pictures and other visual illustrations that you can utilize
Narrative techniques (story-telling) that you employ and repeat
Key words and phrases from other languages that fit contexts
Audio support from recordings, videos, music

Pictures and other illustrations, including manipulatives and realia, help you to build word knowledge because they provide students with the contexts they need for comprehension. Your challenge is to find good ones that correlate with the topics and themes of your instruction and your students' endeavors and then to fold them into your communication. Using the English words associated with these—clearly, repeatedly—helps build word familiarity especially if you emphasize these words, build a "word wall," and re-utilize these words in new contexts and in subsequent lessons.

Incorporate manipulatives and realia into the contexts of new words. Ask students to model the uses of new words, to create new sentences with these words, and to use them as answers to questions that you compose for this purpose. Send students into new situations (the library, a store, home) with the task of using those words. Have them report back to their group or to the class.

Narrative techniques—successful ones that become part of your communication skills—result from planning and practice. As you become adept at focusing students' attentions on new words, you can move from visual representations into narratives such as telling a brief story related to a new word or concept. Most useful, however, is transferring narrative techniques into students' hands— that is, direct students to model the uses of words and phrases, to create new contexts (little stories) for these new words, and to have them speak these to each other.

Many teachers have had success working on language in pair-shares or in small groups. Try asking student pairs to speak in two languages with each other, such as student #1 asking a question in English to be answered by #2 in his or her primary language, and vice versa. Develop your interactions with students and increase the intensity of student-to-student interactions by preparing questions that access students' prior knowledge and that help them put words to their ideas and feelings and other personal connections.

Once you have success with narrative techniques, you can expand into more focused kinds of activities, such as having students in pairs or groups build a story around some stimuli like a visual or a song, a poem or a story.

Key words from students' first languages may be a challenge to identify so this will require research on your part early in the year or prior to work on a particular topic or theme. But it may pay off because it can represent direct linkages between the familiar and the new, especially for students who feel overwhelmed by English. In fact, they may catch on that you care enough to learn about them, and that may help overcome a world of obstacles.

Step one is to identify and collect those words. How do you do that? One obvious way is to schedule a conference with parents of your ELL students, providing they speak English to the extent that you will need. Alternatively, schedule a brief interview with someone in your school or community who is familiar with the language(s) involved. With your next lesson topic or theme in mind, ask for words and phrases that relate directly.

Using those words, however, requires some surgery because you will need to look closely at the content of your lesson or unit. Specifically, you must identify the precise English words or phrases in your content that you can associate with the new words you have discovered. Or you can start with words you've gathered from family or interviewees, and work backwards into your content for appropriate connections. Craft sentences for concept demonstrations, and craft questions about the content—all with a view toward aligning English terms with the ones you've gathered.

Audio support, like visual support, generally increases cognition by associating sounds with words, not only for pronunciation but also for literal meanings and completions of ideas. Music, songs, recorded narratives and conversations—all have a place in your approach to language development.

Support Development of English Proficiency

Make your classroom friendly to your students' various languages while connecting to English. How? Bring elements and examples of those languages into your room via word walls and other kinds of visuals. You will find examples from your research, notably from the key words and phrases you elicit from your students and their families. Consider using a system of color-coding for the different languages, keeping examples of each language true to a designated color. An important goal is to create patterns, or a system, for the various languages in your room that create connections between those focal points and English so that students increase their understanding, their vocabulary (in both their languages perhaps), and their oral and written communication skills.

Repetition is important. As you practice story telling (with younger students), and as you elicit conversations and other student responses, you are making your environment intimately supportive of language development.

In addition to creating a supportive environment, be sure to adapt your instructional approaches accordingly:

- Incorporate key words and phrases from the other languages into your instruction and your questioning so that you leverage their meanings into familiarity with English.
- Make use of small groups and pair-shares that require communication among students.
- Bring audio and visual support into daily activity that illustrates concepts and ideas.
- Utilize your audio and visuals, realia, and other props in ways that encourage students to respond actively.
- Also known as Total Physical Response (TPR), activities that require active student engagement increase the likelihood of learning and retaining language.

- When possible, encourage community members and volunteers familiar with your classroom cultures to participate.

Consult Experts

1. "English Language Development." *Teaching Tools.* www.tkcalifornia. org., 2016. online

2. Forlini, G., Williams, E., and Brinkman, A. *Class Acts: Your Guide To Activate Learning.* Bronxville, New York: Lavender Hill Press, 2016.

3. Gardner, H. *Multiple Intelligences: The Theory in Practice.* New York, NY: Basic Books, 1993.

4. Paul, A. M. "How the Power of Interest Drives Learning." *Mind/Shift: How we will learn.* https://ww2.kqed.org/mindshift/2013/11/04/how-the-power-of-interest-drives-learning, 2013. online

5. Tomlinson, C. A. *The Differentiated Classroom: Responding to the Needs of All Learners.* Alexandria, VA: ASCD, 2014.

6. Turner, M. J. and Hope, K. *How the Right Brain Learns.* Sidney, BC: Ardmore Pub., 2010.

Self Assess: Focusing on Student Needs

For each element, self-assess using the following 1-4 scale:

1. **Missing (I need to do this)**
2. **Attempted (I try to do this, but I am not successful)**
3. **Apparent (I do this well, but I don't do it consistently. When I do it, it works!)**
4. **Well Done (I do this consistently and appropriately)**

Group Students and Design Curriculum for Differentiated Learning   1   2   3   4

I can answer the following questions before I begin a lesson:
Who needs more background knowledge before I begin this lesson?
Who already knows what I am about to teach?
Who is just ready for this content?

Provide Ongoing Assessment To Inform Teaching and Learning   1   2   3   4

I frequently use pre-assessment, real-time assessment, and post-assessment to inform my planning of differentiated learning experiences.

Respond to Student Differences
My pre-assessment gives me data to tailor instruction,
while my mid- and post-assessments help me to …

Develop Varied Learning Goals.   1 2 3 4
I develop varied learning goals according to the
needs of individual students.

Set Varied Lesson Pacing.   1 2 3 4
I set varied lesson pace according to the needs
of individual students.

Select Varied Materials.   1 2 3 4
I use varied learning resources according to
the needs of individual students.

Choose a Mode of Teaching.   1 2 3 4
I select from a variety of teaching techniques (direct
instruction, inquiry-based instruction, cooperative
learning, problem-based learning, self-directed learning,
and others) to deliver instruction that will meet
varied student needs.

Use Flexible Grouping.   1 2 3 4
I group students according to interests, skill levels,
prior knowledge, previous performance, concept
understanding, depth of knowledge, needs determined
by assessments and more.

Differentiate Through Content   1 2 3 4
I modify content by varying the depth and complexity.

Differentiate Through Process   1 2 3 4
I modify the process by varying the higher-level
thinking processes.

Differentiate Through Product   1 2 3 4
I modify product by varying the way students demonstrate
their knowledge.

Design Differentiated Lessons   1 2 3 4
I design effective differentiated lessons to meet the
individual needs of my students.

Incorporate Tools of Language Development   1 2 3 4
I incorporate the following into my introduction of new words:

• Pictures and other illustrations
• Narrative techniques
• Key words from students' first languages

Designing the canals of Amsterdam presented urban planners with an enormous challenge. Facing swamps and a largely undeveloped landscape, engineers unpacked the cultural and technical challenges involved, including mechanics of river flow, so that they could design networks of waterways in combination with urban streets and buildings—all planned in stages to reach their desired outcome of a new port city central to European commerce and trade.

Construct Learning around Curriculum Requirements

objectives ... targets ... outcomes

On Mary Pat's team was Gil Kelton, a science specialist whom she found enormously resourceful, if a bit verbose. Although Gil was nearing retirement, she knew, his excitement about planning never seemed to flag, and his ideas for developing his plans were endless.

When Mary Pat mentioned to Gil that she struggled with a certain math curriculum standard, he considered that a worthy challenge and so he launched full steam into the nuts, bolts, and underlying philosophy of developing learning. "Keep your eye on the ball," he began. "Study it. Know where you are going."

Be Clear about State or District Standards

So Gil began at the very core of planning. "Normally, a state or district standard contains levels of increasingly specific concepts and skills that your students must master." And he offered Mary Pat this example from his science standards:

STANDARD I: Students will understand that water changes state as it moves through the water cycle.

Objective 1: Describe the relationship between heat energy, evaporation and condensation of water on Earth.

Objective 2: Describe the water cycle.

a. Locate examples of evaporation and condensation in the water cycle (e.g., water evaporates when heated and clouds or dew forms when vapor is cooled).

b. Describe the processes of evaporation, condensation, and precipitation as they relate to the water cycle.

c. Identify locations that hold water as it passes through the water cycle (e.g., oceans, atmosphere, fresh surface water, snow, ice, and ground water).

d. Construct a model or diagram to show how water continuously moves through the water cycle over time.

e. Describe how the water cycle relates to the water supply in your community.

"I begin by narrowing those concepts and skills into lesson chunks," he said, "which become my learning targets for students. You can do this, too. Start by understanding what to look for inside the standard, the intended outcome and your objective for the lesson."

Focus Your Understanding as You Unpack a Standard	
Outcome	what a learning standard indicates that students should know and be able to do.
Objective	what students should know and do regarding a *major portion* of a standard.
Learning Target	what *you* focus on and articulate for students in specific lesson chunks. Your learning targets are what you plan specifically for students to know and to do as a result of a single lesson.

Plan Instruction from Core Standards

"To help *all* of your students master essential knowledge and skills," Gil said, "you first must clarify *for yourself* what students must know and be able to do as a result of instruction." He pointed out that researchers tell us that teachers who create clarity for themselves are teachers who achieve greater academic gains. [1,2,3]

To create clarity, a teacher must increase his understanding of, and his focus on, approved curriculum core standards and the concepts and skills contained therein. It may require reading and rereading, particularly if a standard is broad or challenging. This is important because close analysis of the ideas within a standard helps you focus your own thinking, which leads to your well articulated learning outcomes and plans. Your task, then, is to sharpen your understanding of a specific standard or concept so that you can formulate precise, lesson-sized concepts and skills that your students will understand. Once they understand, you and they have a better chance of mastering the concept together.

Gil offered an example to show how teachers can clarify precisely what students need to know and be able to do, and he explained that researchers have developed a useful process. "Here is a two-stage process they suggest," he said.

Two Stage Process for Developing Learning Outcomes for Students
Stage One: Analyze a core standard to identify its essential concept(s) and skill(s). **TO DO:** *Read and re-read. Underline key concept(s). Bold each skill.*
Stage Two: Create your learning outcomes (for students) by changing the language of the concept and/or skill(s) into wording that you believe students will understand. **TO DO:** *Rewrite key concepts and skills into new wording for students.*

Focus Your Learning Objectives

Gil used an example to demonstrate Stage One. "Look how the teacher analyzes one of his science standards. He <u>underlines</u> three key concepts within the standard (notice that these are nouns, noun phrases, or clauses), and then he **bolds** three verbs that express the specific skills, or tasks, that students must master:

Standard 1, Objective 2: Students **will understand** that <u>water changes state as it moves through the water cycle.</u>

    a. **Locate** examples of <u>evaporation and condensation</u> in the water cycle (e.g., water evaporates when heated and clouds or dew forms when vapor cools).

    b. **Describe** the <u>process of evaporation, transpiration, condensation, and precipitation</u> as they relate to <u>the water cycle.</u>

"Think of your analysis as a search for <u>content</u> (which are science concepts, in this case), and think of your analysis also as a search for skills (best expressed by verbs) that students must perform."

Gil continued, "Then the teacher <u>underlines</u> science concepts that students must encounter, perhaps in a diagram or an experiment. Your challenge begins with thinking and focusing on those specific concepts (evaporation, condensation). How will you demonstrate those for students? What words will you use to discuss those?

"Notice also that the teacher **bolds** key words—all of them verbs—that represent the skills that students must master." Gil explained that typically, a standard contains such words as indicators of the kinds of performance, or actions, that students must perform and master. Those verbs contain signals for you because each verb reveals the depths of knowledge and skills required of students and implies what will be required of you to help students access the knowledge and skills. A verb like **locate**, for instance, means "find," which is a fairly straight-forward action, and it implies that you must direct students to a location such as a diagram where they can find something meaningful. A verb like **describe**, on the other hand, requires deeper thought because this action requires detailed understanding of something that they locate, or find.

Thus far, you have thought about the concepts you must help students approach and engage, and you have identified actions that you want students to make. Another way to focus on these as you plan a lesson is to make a graphic organizer for yourself. Here's one that juxtaposes the concepts alongside the skills:

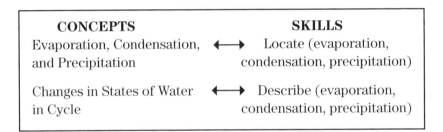

Notice that the skills relate directly to the concepts (communicated by nouns); in fact, the skills help reveal the concepts because other key words (expressed by verbs) are precise vehicles for engaging students in the skills within the concepts. This kind of planning can make your activities and directions most effective because the wording that you choose will help students engage intimately with the concepts. The sharpest verbs complemented by the most relevant nouns and pronouns can be your roadmap for students.

Focus Outcomes To Articulate Student Learning Targets

State or district standards contain objectives, which are written for teachers to describe the knowledge and skills that would likely take students several lessons to learn. However, you must develop learning targets—each a statement that you write for students to articulate a lesson-sized chunk of knowledge and skills that you want them to master.[2] In other words, your learning targets will express to students exactly what you want them to learn in a single lesson.

"In Stage Two," Gil explained, "your best learning target statement will also convey how deeply your students must delve and how they will demonstrate mastery."

Simply put, a teacher increases learning first by focusing for himself what he expects (in terms of specific content-area concepts and skills) and then by articulating those expectations in student-friendly language that is designed (by you, the teacher) to make student performance clear and understandable (to them). This requires a little work (by you).[4]

The teacher who unpacked the concept and skills in the previous charts proceeded then to formulate more specific outcomes and objectives, as you can see next. The teacher recognized that he will need several lessons to cover the objective.

Articulation Plan for Standard 1, Objective 2	
Students will understand that water changes state as it moves through the water cycle	
My Learning Outcomes / Expectations	**Student Learning Targets**
Day One:	Day One:
1. Students will understand what evaporation means.	1. I can find definitions of evaporation in the water cycle diagram.
2. *They will recognize examples of evaporation in the water cycle.*	2. *I can label evaporation in the correct places in the water cycle diagram.*
3. They will describe the evaporation process in the water cycle.	3. I can tell my lab partner what happens to water during evaporation.
4. *Students will understand that water changes state as it moves through the cycle.*	4. *I can make my own diagram of the water cycle showing evaporation.*

Day Two:	Day Two:
5. Students will understand what condensation means.	5. I can find definitions of condensation in the water cycle diagram.
6. *They will recognize examples of condensation in the water cycle.*	6. *I can label condensation in the correct places in the water cycle diagram.*
7. They will describe the condensation process in the water cycle.	7. I can tell my lab partner what happens to water during condensation.
8. *Students will understand that water changes state as it moves through the cycle.*	8. *I can make my own diagram of the water cycle showing evaporation.*
Day Three:	Day Three:
9. Students will understand what precipitation means.	9. I can find definitions of precipitation in the water cycle diagram.
... and so forth.	... and so forth.

Assess Students' Developing Understanding during Instruction

While you perform this kind of word-smithing in your own planning, keep one more thing in mind: the learning targets that you create can serve also as indicators of each student's developing mastery during the lesson process. Not only are you focusing learning objectives, you also are creating embedded assessments, which will be useful to you and to students as you together move through the lesson process. What does that mean?

It means that a well-crafted learning objective (*In the Water Cycle chart, locate an example of evaporation*) gives you an assessment measure (*student finds it or he doesn't*) and it gives your student a yardstick for self-analysis (*I see it or I don't see it*).

Many researchers refer to this process of assessing students' developing mastery during a lesson as "Performances of Understanding"[2] while some others call it "Embedded Formative Assessment."[3] Data that you gather from this formative assessment process enable you to adjust the pace of your lesson, to adapt your lesson to better meet your students' developing needs, and to provide extra assistance to students who struggle to master the lesson-sized chunks of concepts and skills. Researchers have found that embedding formative assessments that position you to adjust your instruction in real time to student needs is the most effective strategy to increase learning.[5] Communicating to students how they will demonstrate their developing mastery during the lesson further clarifies what they will need to know and be able to do as a result of the lesson.

Give Look-Fors to Students

Part of communicating learning objectives to students is clarifying what to look for as they engage with your lesson, which helps them self-monitor their progress. You can give students concrete markers to support your learning target. For instance, you might tell students that they will be succeeding when they can correctly place labels on a diagram to show where evaporation, condensation, and precipitation occur.

Four Steps To Consider

Keep in mind a simple sequence of steps that you can follow once you have clarified learning outcomes (for yourself) and you have focused learning objectives (for students).

STEP ONE: **Present and Display Outcomes and Objectives.**
Explain to students what they will be learning from this single lesson by using your understanding of the key concepts and skills in the standard. Be sure to post or display the learning objectives.

STEP TWO: **Orient Students to Tasks Ahead.**
Tell students how they will demonstrate their developing mastery of the skills within the learning objectives. Refer to those you have posted or displayed regularly.

STEP THREE: **Describe *Look-Fors* to Students.**
Share indicators of mastery that students can look for to monitor their own growing understanding and mastery.

STEP FOUR: **Expand with The Big Picture.**
Explain to students why these concepts and skills are relevant to their lives and why they are important to learn.

Consult Experts

1. Ainsworth, L. and Viegut D. *Common Formative Assessments: How to Connect Standards-based Instruction and Assessment.* Thousand Oaks, CA: Corwin Press, 2006.

2. Moss, C. M., Brookhart S.M., and Association for Supervision and Curriculum Development. *Learning Targets: Helping Students Aim for Understanding in Today's Lesson.* Alexandria, VA: ASCD, 2012.

3. Wiliam, D. *Embedded Formative Assessment.* Bloomington, IN: Solution Tree Press, 2011.

4. Forlini, G., Williams, E., and Brinkman, A. *Class Acts: Your Guide To Activate Learning.* Bronxville, NY: Lavender Hill Press, 2016.

5. Popham, W. J. *Transformative Assessment in Action: An Inside Look at Applying the Process.* Alexandria, VA: ASCD, 2011.

6. Moss, C.M., Brookhart, S.M., and Long, B.A. "Knowing Your Learning Target." *Educational Leadership* 68 (6), 2011.

Self Assess: Setting Instructional Outcomes

For each element, self-assess using the following 1-4 scale:

1. Missing (I need to do this)
2. Attempted (I try to do this, but I am not successful)
**3. Apparent (I do this well, but I don't do it consistently.
   When I do it, it works!)**
4. Well Done (I do this consistently and appropriately)

Clarifying My Learning Targets   1 2 3 4

I draw my learning targets from a concept and/or skill derived
from a core standard, which I have analyzed.

Focusing My Learning Targets   1 2 3 4

My learning targets focus on only one lesson-sized chunk
of concepts and skills.

Displaying Learning Targets   1 2 3 4

I display my learning targets visually and present them to
my students by explaining what they will be learning.

Communicating Learning Targets   1 2 3 4

I explain to students why these concepts and skills are
relevant to their lives and important to learn.

Designing Assessments   1 2 3 4

I design several ways for my students to demonstrate
developing mastery.

Communicating Assessments   1 2 3 4

I tell students how they will demonstrate their
developing mastery.

Guiding for Understanding   1 2 3 4

I identify a set of look-fors, or criteria of understanding,
that I can share with my students so they can monitor
their own growth toward mastery.

Explaining The Big Picture   1 2 3 4

I explain to students why these concepts and skills are
relevant to their lives and important to learn.

Assess. Assess. Assess. Success depends on it. Product builders and service providers use specialists to assess the status and needs of their constituents. The specialists design assessment forms like questionnaires, product tests, focus groups, audience participation techniques, and satisfaction surveys to gain knowledge to inform the builders and providers. They know that improvements result from the information gained through carefully constructed assessment vehicles.

Draw Up
Assessment Protocols

assessments ... interventions ... adjustments

By the time principal Lacey held her first formal staff meeting on an in-service day about formative assessment, Mary Pat and Clay already had been planning for it. They met informally on several occasions with language arts teacher Dan Vernier from Mary Pat's interdisciplinary team as well as another member of Mary Pat's math team, Marge Quimby.

It was no secret that Ms. Lacey would expect her goal to be met in concrete, content-specific, and research-based ways, and so many on the faculty looked closely at their own past and current protocols for using assessments. Many were nervous about it because they had developed their assessments independently, without review, while some admitted confusion about the effectiveness of their formative assessment devices, or lack thereof.

Viola recognized her staff's anxiety about the efficacy of their past efforts, and when she learned from Clay about the informal discussions happening in the various teams, she wisely invited members of Mary Pat's teams to set the stage for the first meeting.

Incorporate Actionable Formative Assessments

"First, let's understand where Common Formative Assessments (CFAs) fit in the process of collaborating to maximize student learning," Viola began. "Once you have unpacked a standard with your team so that you can target specific concepts and skills, you will develop a Pre-CFA that each team member will administer to his or her students. This may be a kind of test or activity that assesses each of the concepts and skills within the standard. Your Pre-CFA, then, will give you feedback from students from which you and your team determine mastery levels for each student before any first-time instruction takes place."

First to jump in was Dan Vernier. He came to the meeting prepared with data displays from a 6th grade language arts class. He pointed out that a Pre-CFA yields very important data. How you display that data is a critical team function. For instance, as a team, you might identify your method of deciding if a student has mastered a specific concept or skill, if s/he is below mastery, or approaching mastery.

You use the data display from your Pre-CFA to help plan first-time instruction related to each concept and skill by identifying patterns in the data and by using protocols to differentiate instruction.

Later, once you teach those essential concepts and skills, you are ready to use a Post-CFA, which your team has developed, to measure students' relative degrees of mastery *following* your first-time teaching. Often, a team will develop the Pre- and Post-CFAs concurrently to ensure using the same patterns of assessment in each. "That's what I did, which I'll show you in a moment," Dan said.

"Again, each team member develops a data display—this time from their Post-CFAs—and then analyzes the data. Here the rubber really meets the road, because the patterns and points of information in the data point you toward specific interventions for students who did not achieve mastery from first-time teaching, as well as re-teaching of concepts and skills for other students who are approaching mastery and enrichment for those students who have mastered concepts and skills within the standard."

Dan projected his data display for the staff to examine.

"It's one thing to agree that data-by-student and data-by-skill are useful information," he continued, "but it's quite another to know exactly how to gather and present such information.

"Here is an example of data that I collected to show the results of my formative assessment. My lesson was about writing argument, part of a series of lessons I gave on developing an essay that uses persuasion to convince readers of an argument, a position. As you probably know, these concepts and skills are part of our state's writing standard about argumentation."

Dan walked the group through his data, which displays the concepts and skills within the standard (across the top of the table) along with student level of mastery (below, approaching, mastering) displayed down the page beneath each concept and skill:

My Data Display PRE-Common Formative Assessment: Argumentation Standard						
Student	Introduces Topic	Makes a Claim	Supports Claim with Reasons and Facts	Presents an Opposing Argument	Refutes Opposing Argument with Facts, Reasons	Makes a Summary that Leads to a Conclusion
Lisa Short	Below	Below	Below	Below	Below	Below
Charles Allent	Below	Below	Below	Below	Below	Below

continued on next page

Lucy Smith	Below	Below	Approach	Below	Below	Below
Juan Diego	Approach	Approach	Approach	Below	Below	Below
Louis Garcia	Approach	Approach	Approach	Below	Below	Below
Shaun Jones	Approach	Approach	Below	Below	Below	Below
Rich Roan	Approach	Approach	Approach	Below	Below	Below
Soren Jensen	Master	Approach	Approach	Below	Below	Below
Star Orullian	Master	Master	Master	Master	Approach	Approach
John Jansen	Master	Master	Master	Master	Master	Approach
Thuyne Du	Master	Master	Master	Master	Master	Master

"Once we shared our pre-common formative assessments," Dan said, "the team went further to develop specific questions to help us locate and analyze patterns revealed by the shared data. We analyzed the data at the concept/skill level and then at the student level, and we noted the numbers of students who mastered, approached mastery, and fell short of mastering each concept and skill."

It was clear to Dan's team that the areas likely requiring the deepest teaching are presenting arguments, refuting arguments, and making a successful conclusion for an argument (See the last 3 columns in Dan's display.).

Although the team used a graphic scheme, they could also have used color-coding to help distinguish patterns.

Remember this: The purpose of collaborative analysis of pre-common formative assessment data is to plan differentiated first-time instruction tailored to students' needs.

And this: As you meet as a team to analyze pre-common formative assessment data, think about tapping into school resources such as the media specialist for materials and the special education teacher for students who have Individual Education Plans (IEPs).

Dan's team devised the following note-taking guide in three columns. The first identifies important questions to ask about the data. The second column documents the patterns that emerge. And the third records actions that team members decide to take in response to the patterns.

As Dan displayed his example to the faculty, he underscored this point: **"These actions (analyzing the data and recording your observations) lead you toward differentiating your strategies for individual students."** Here is what he displayed:

Our Data Analysis: Pre-Common Formative Assessment		
Questions	Findings	Actions
What patterns emerge at the concept/ skill level?	1. 70% of students have mastered or are approaching grade-level mastery of: • Introducing a Topic, • Making a Claim, and • Supporting a Claim with Reasons and Facts 2. 30% of students fall below grade level on those three concepts/ skills.	1. Give a short review of these 3 concepts to all students followed by an embedded assessment that measures each student's ability to introduce a topic, make a claim, and support a claim with reasons and facts. 2. Give independent two-tiered assignment that is at grade level and beyond grade level. 3. Provide strategic small group instruction based on insights from embedded assessments after group instruction.
	1. 70% of students scored below grade level on • Present an Opposing Argument, • Refute Opposing Argument with Facts and Reasons, and • Make a Summary that Leads to a Conclusion. 2. 30% of students approached mastery or have mastered.	1a. Allocate the greatest amount of instructional time to focus on these three concepts. 1b. Use explicit instruction to scaffold the learning for students. 1c. Use engagement requests to get all students thinking about and applying concepts.

continued on next page

What are the patterns at the student level?	1. Students who scored below in nearly every concept/skill: Lisa, Charles, and Lucy 2. Students who demonstrated mastery in nearly every concept/skill: John, Thuyen 3. Students who demonstrated they are on track to master all concepts/skills during scheduled time: Juan, Louis, Shaun, Rich, Soren, Star	1. Provide instruction at 3 levels: Pre-teach (start with concepts below grade level), whole group (grade level concepts), small group (level determined by embedded assessment given during whole group). 2. Extend instruction and independent assignments to argumentation concepts/skills for next grade level above. 3. Provide grade level instruction integrating continuous embedded assessment throughout instruction.

"At the end of our period of first-time instruction," Dan continued his presentation, "each of us gave our students a post common formative assessment so that we could design precise interventions for students who didn't achieve mastery, enrichment for students who did demonstrate mastery, and large-group re-teaching of concepts and skills that most students failed to master."

He projected another example for the group to see. "Notice that we have organized our post-common formative assessment to be similar to our pre-common assessment. Specifically, the Post-Common Formative Assessment shows the progress made by each student for each concept and skill within the standard."

My POST-Common Formative Assessment: Argumentation Standard						
Student	Introduces Topic	Makes a Claim	Supports Claim with Reasons and Facts	Presents an Opposing Argument	Refutes Opposing Argument with Facts, Reasons	Makes a Summary that Leads to a Conclusion
Color-Codes	Below Master		Approach		Master	
Lisa Short	Master	Master	Approach	Approach	Below	Below

continued on next page

Charles Allent	Master	Master	Master	Master	Approach	Below
Lucy Smith	Master	Master	Master	Master	Approach	Below
Juan Diego	Master	Master	Master	Master	Approach	Below
Louis Garcia	Master	Master	Master	Master	Approach	Below
Shaun Jones	Master	Master	Master	Master	Approach	Approach
Rich Roan	Master	Master	Master	Master	Master	Approach
Soren Jensen	Master	Master	Master	Master	Master	Approach
Star Orullian	Master	Master	Master	Master	Master	Approach
John Jansen	Master	Master	Master	Master	Master	Master
Thuyne Du	Master	Master	Master	Master	Master	Master

Move Toward Interventions and Other Learning Opportunities

After the faculty had time to discuss Dan's pre- and post-CFAs, Mary Pat and Marge Quimby introduced the tactic of organizing the data into useful parts by devising questions that would lead toward specific actions.

"To analyze our data, we asked ourselves 'In what different ways can this data help us as we move forward with our students?'" Mary Pat continued, "We identified three types of analyses that would tell us the most. First, what do we learn about the Concept/Skill Level? That is, which of the concepts and skills did students master and which ones didn't they?

"Second, on the Student Level, which students need re-teaching and on which skills?

"And, third, on the Instructional Practices Level, what do we as teachers need to consider and re-consider about our instructional methods?"

"What I like so much about this," Viola interjected, "is that it lays out a PLAN, and the plan leads to specific interventions for students who have not mastered the concepts and skills."

When the team displayed their complete Data Analysis, Dan led the group through the specific questions they had devised for each section of data (their Inquiry Questions, left column), what the data revealed to them about each question (middle column), and the specific actions that Dan identified for his students.

Our Data Analysis: POST-Common Formative Assessment		
Inquiry Questions	Findings	Actions
Analysis at the Concept/Skill Level		
1. Which concepts/skills were mastered by 90% or above?	1. Introduce Topic, Make a Claim, Support Claim with Reasons/Facts, Present Opposing Argument.	1. Celebrate!!!!
2. Which concepts/skills should be retaught to nearly the whole group?	2. Make Summary that leads to a conclusion; students can summarize, but are not able to use that summary to derive a conclusion.	2a. Each teacher re-teaches to all students below mastery with an emphasis on making summary lead to a conclusion. 2b. Will develop common lesson-plans to focus on conclusion.
3. Which concepts/skills should be re-taught to small groups to be constituted strategically?	3. Refute Opposing Arguments with Facts and Reasons.	3a. Regroup students across grade level, each taught by one teacher: • Students below standard • Students approaching standard • Students who mastered 3b. Reteach this concept/ skill during daily 20 minute re-teach/ enrich slot. Focus instruction on crafting a conclusion.

continued on next page

Analysis at the Student Level		
4. Which students require re-teaching and on what concept/skills?	4a. Lisa, Charles, Lucy, Juan, Louis, Shaun – Refute Opposing Arguments w/Facts and Reasons 4b. Lisa needs re-teaching on: • Support Claim • Present Opposing Argument • Refute Opposing Argument • Make Summary Conclusion	4. Reteach concepts/skills as per findings.
5. Which students require no re-teaching and should be provided with extension and enrichment?	5a. John, Thuyne 5b. Rich, Soren, Star	
Reflect on Effectiveness of Instructional Practices		
6. Based on the data, which of our instructional methods were strong?	• Analyze strategically selected commercials & identify claim & support. • Create commercials that refute the selected commercial. • Webbing/Graphic Organizers. • Student-to-student line talk using graphic organizer to present their claim and support.	
7. Which strategies are weak? In what ways might we strengthen our instructional approach for re-teaching the concept/skill on which the majority of students failed to achieve mastery?	Summary that leads to a conclusion.	Make a common series of lessons that focus on making a summary that leads to a conclusion, especially helping students understand what a conclusion is: • Have students examine effective models of summaries that lead to a conclusion. • Use think alouds to model crafting summary that leads to conclusion. • And so forth….

Dan made a final point that one's analysis is not complete without considering the use of school resource personnel such as the media specialist, a special ed teacher, para-professional, and possibly parent volunteers.

And the point of all this: Your answers to post-CFA questions provide rich information that teams can use to design precise interventions to help students who don't achieve mastery of essentials the first time. With this information, teams can also identify and provide extended learning opportunities for students who mastered essentials. By reflecting on data that shows which standards most students did or did not pass after first-time instruction, teams can identify methods that were effective and those that need to be strengthened. These teams then can collaborate to strengthen practices they deemed weak. This strengthening process is one of teachers' best sources for developing new knowledge of instructional practice.

Follow a Tight Formative Assessment Process

Formative Assessment is a planned, action-oriented process in which the classroom teacher collects evidence of student learning at key junctures as teaching and learning unfold using that data to make decisions about the next instructional steps to take.[9]

Successful Formative Assessment increases learning outcomes for students, for sure, yet it also changes the classroom climate in dramatic and positive ways. At its best, the formative assessment PROCESS shifts student awareness away from an interest only in grades and toward a focus on learning and mastering.

Leading experts in educational assessment like James Popham offer steps that you can take to plan and integrate formative assessment into your instructional practice.[9] Your challenge is to master such a PROCESS if you have not already done so, or to sharpen the process in your practice. Its steps are clear while offering you the opportunity to engage your planning skills and your knowledge of the content you teach.

Every time you approach Formative Assessment, you can start here:

Understand your targeted learning outcome—thoroughly. It may derive from a core curriculum standard or other objective and includes specific concepts and skills. Your instructional plan to reach that outcome may be a single lesson or a series of lessons depending on its complexity. Be sure that you clearly understand what students need to learn (specific concepts and skills) and when you expect them to master those concepts and skills (e.g., a single lesson, several days of lessons, a unit or full standard over a certain period of time).

Develop a Learning Progression To Plan the Timing of Your Formative Assessments. You first need to develop a learning progression, which consists of sub-skills and chunks of enabling knowledge sequenced in the logical order that leads students to gain understanding and/or information so that they progress toward mastering the intended learning outcome.

Think of this as a three-part process:

Develop a Learning Progression
Part 1: Perform a task analysis of the learning outcome.
Part 2: Order the blocks of sub-skills and enabling knowledge into a logical sequence.
Part 3: Identify sub-skills and enabling knowledge that are measurable.

Following is a research-based protocol that further explains the process of developing a learning progression:

Process for Developing a Learning Progression

Part 1: Perform a task analysis of the learning outcome. Use your judgment to determine what sub-skills and bodies of enabling knowledge students must understand and be able to do to achieve mastery of the whole learning outcome. Be guided by the following definitions:

> A **sub-skill** is a simple, specific ability students must develop in order to go onto a more complex one.

> A chunk of **enabling knowledge** is information or understandings of ideas that students must possess to successfully master the learning outcome.

Together, each sub-skill and chunk of enabling knowledge comprise the learning outcome that students must learn in order to achieve the entire learning outcome.

Part 2: Order the blocks of sub-skills and enabling knowledge into a logical sequence. Place the blocks of sub-skills and chunks of enabling knowledge in an instructional sequence that represents the logical order in which students must learn them to master the whole learning outcome. This ordering is not an exact science; it represents your judgment of what students must learn first, then second, and so forth as they progress toward attaining the whole learning outcome. This sequencing process is how you scaffold the learning to help students move from "not knowing" to "knowing" or from "not being able to do" to "being able to do." Sub-skills and chunks of enabling knowledge that comprise the learning progression work interdependently as students move up the ladder from the simplest to most complex.

Part 3: Identify sub-skills and enabling knowledge that are measurable. Evaluate each sub-skill or chunk of enabling knowledge to see if it is measurable. Better still, when selecting sub-skills and chunks of enabling knowledge for the learning progression, look for those that are measurable because it is at these junctures that you administer formative assessments to gather evidence of students' learning status.

Plan your Formative Assessments. Once you've built your learning progression, you can plan your formative assessments. For each measurable sub-skill or chunk of enabling knowledge, you can determine a small task or brief test from which you can collect assessment-derived data that will reveal to you the mastery level of each student—at that juncture.

Make Adjustment Decisions. This is a critical juncture for you as well as for your students. Not only will you learn how each student has progressed—his or her level of understanding, misperceptions, and specific needs—but also you gain a roadmap for adjusting your instruction.

For instance, if you find evidence that most students have <u>not</u> mastered a sub-skill or block of enabling knowledge within the learning progression, then you might loop back to re-teach those concepts and skills. On the other hand, if your formative assessment shows that most have mastered it, then you might review it briefly and spend more time on the next chunk of learning. And in either scenario, you can identify individuals who perform differently from most other students, and for them you can provide intervention or enrichment.

Craft Your Formative Assessments Wisely

Selecting the right type of assessment for each sub-block of **enabling knowledge** and skills is critical to getting a true picture of students' developing abilities. You have many options open to you, and you will likely choose from among those as you gain insight into the needs of your students as well as the types of inquiries and activities that elicit the most useful data.

In addition to traditional assessment methods, consider using "all respond" techniques because you can integrate these easily into a lesson. Such activities can give you a quick picture of students' learning status. Resources such as those by Himmele & Himmele, Wiliam, and Popham offer many and varied ideas for formative assessments which permit teachers to address the different learning styles of students. [7,9,10] Here are a few:

All-Respond Techniques

1. **Letter- or number- card responses** call for each student to be given a set of 3-4 cards, each of which has a letter on one side and a number on the other. For example, one card may have the letter A on one side and the number 1 on the other. The next card would have the letter B on one side and the number 2 on the other side, and so forth. The teacher frames a multiple-choice question that offers students 3-4 options. First, the teacher poses the question; next s/he presents 3-4 options (listed on board or projected on a screen); then, s/he has students select the card with the correct letter or number; and finally, s/he signals for all students to hold up their cards at the same time. The teacher quickly scans students' responses to discern if they are getting it and, if not, what are the main misunderstandings?

2. **Response Boards** are small erasable white boards (roughly 8 by 12 inches) given to each student to record responses to assessment questions. Response boards can also be made by laminating each side of a piece of card stock. For both types, students can use pieces of cloth to clear the board. Response boards are more flexible in that they offer a greater menu of student responses, such as working a math problem, visually representing a story problem, writing a word, crafting a sentence, and drawing a quick diagram or picture. However, the process is similar to the card responses. The teacher presents the question to which all students record their responses and then hold them up on the teacher's signal. The teacher scrutinizes student responses to proceed to, or adjust, the next instructional step.

3. **Physical Responses** provide additional ways all students can respond, such as Thumbs up Thumbs down, hands on head (ear, temple…), move to a particular part of the room, act out a meaning to a word, and so forth.

You might also consider using **Student Self-Assessments**, which ask students to monitor and reflect upon their own developing mastery. This nurtures an awareness of self-as-learner, and it connects students with ways in which their learning tactics affect their learning. Also, it triggers their desire to select learning tactics consciously to enhance their ability to master essentials.

Student Self-Assessments

1. **Traffic-Signal Techniques**, such as this one from James Popham, provide students with viable ways to commun-cate to their teacher their perceived level of understanding of the focus sub-block of learning.

   All students have three stacked cups, each a different color. For example, a red cup might indicate total confusion, a yellow cup may represent developing understanding, and a green cup may signal mastery. During the teacher's instruc-tion, students place the colored cup on top of the stack that best represents their level of understanding. The teacher can monitor these cups during instruction, using the changing colors of the top cups to determine if and when adjustments are called for. An example would be, if after instructing on a building block of enabling knowledge or sub-skill, the teacher notices that most of the cups are red, that might spark the decision to loop back and re-teach the same enabling knowledge and sub-skills using different methods. Or the teacher might decide to administer a quick assessment to determine with which aspect students are struggling. [9]

2. **Checklists or Rubrics** provide opportunities for students to reflect on indicators of mastery of sub-blocks of enabling knowledge or skills. Beside each indicator, the student records his/her level of understanding. Primary grade students might use a simple smile or frown. Older grades could use a three-point scale, such as a smile, a straight face, or a frown or numbers 1-3 with three being high. For older students, a five-point scale could be used to indicate a more finite level of mastery.

See How Others Crafted Single-Lesson Formative Assessment

One of Viola's seventh grade English teachers began planning lessons for writing explanatory (expository) paragraphs. He deter-mined that he would spend 1 to 2 days on the skills and concepts.

To begin identifying segments in his instruction and segments of student learning, he focused a specific learning outcome—*I can write an explanatory paragraph that will identify essential equipment for a full-day hike*—that would take 1.5 to 2 class periods ending with each student writing an original paragraph of his or her own, probably toward the end of period on the second day.

One-to-Two-Day Lesson: Writing Explanatory Paragraphs

Learning Outcome: *I can write an explanatory paragraph that will identify essential equipment for a full-day hike.*

Realizing that this learning outcome is for two days, he created a learning outcome specifically for the first lesson:

Learning Outcome for Lesson One: Writing Explanatory Paragraphs

I can demonstrate that I understand the parts of and can use a graphic organizer to plan an explanatory paragraph that I will write.

He created a learning progression by analyzing the learning outcome for Lesson One. He began by identifying **sub-skills** and **enabling knowledge** necessary. First, he outlined the knowledge that all students need to know by the end of the first 15 minutes, and then he identified two sub-skills that his students should perform to demonstrate for him that they "get it." Here is the simple learning progression he planned for this lesson:

Body of Enabling Knowledge

An explanatory paragraph includes these elements:
- An interesting topic sentence that introduces the subject.
- A series of supporting examples with identifying details for each.
- Transitional words that connect the supporting examples.
- A concluding sentence or two that refers to the topic and closes the discussion logically.

Sub-Skills for Learning Progression
Sub-Skill #1: Identify each part of an explanatory paragraph.
Sub-Skill #2: Draw a graphic organizer to demonstrate the parts of an explanatory paragraph.

Looking at this learning progression, he saw that he had three junctures at which he could give a formative assessment to gauge students' learning status, and so he planned a formative assessment for the body of enabling knowledge, for sub-skill #1, and for sub-skill #2.

Once he identified his sub-skills and enabling knowledge, the teacher began to craft specific tasks to occur after those first 15 minutes, his first learning progression. Those tasks would be his **formative assessments**. He used a partner-share technique to get quick feedback about the enabling knowledge as well as sub-skill #1, which would include a new context, a paragraph that students haven't seen before. And he decided for sub-skill #2 to have each student work independently to create a graphic organizer while he moved among their desks to observe their product.

The teacher's plan included using the graphic organizers from sub-skill #2 as his springboard to the next day's class session. Each student's graphic organizer would guide him or her into outlining a first draft of the paragraph.

Here schematically are the teacher's formative assessments juxtaposed with the enabling knowledge and sub-skills. Note that the formative assessments include the teacher's attention to materials and procedures:

Paragraph Lessons: Learning Progression #1	
Learning Elements	Formative Assessments
<u>Body of Enabling Knowledge</u> An explanatory paragraph includes these elements: • An interesting topic sentence that introduces the subject. • A series of supporting examples with identifying details for each. • Transitional words that connect the supporting examples. • A concluding sentence or two that refers to the topic and closes the discussion logically.	**Use Partner-Share Technique** **Round 1:** <u>Partner A</u>: Verbally state and describe each element of an effective explanatory paragraph. <u>Partner B:</u> As your partner correctly states and describes each element of an explanatory paragraph, check it off on the check list provided. <u>Partner A:</u> Put your green cup on top of the stack if you performed this task correctly or a yellow cup on top if you described it mostly right. **Round 2:** Change roles and repeat the process.
Sub-Skill #1: Identify each part of an explanatory paragraph.	**Read the explanatory paragraph printed out for you. Use your pencil and the 4 highlighters to mark each of its parts as follows:** **Green** – Topic sentence. **Yellow** – Two examples that support the topic sentence. **Orange** – Two details within each of those examples. **Blue** – Conclusion that refers back to the topic and ties it all together. **Pencil** – Circle 3 transitional words or phrases.
Sub-Skill #2: Draw a graphic organizer to demonstrate the parts of an explanatory paragraph.	Create a graphic organizer for a paragraph you will write about hiking. Label each part of your paragraph. For each part, insert some ideas you will write.

Determine and Refine Your Instructional Adjustments

Done properly, your formative assessments will yield action-able information about each student's progress and will put you into position for making decisions like more instruction or less instruc-tion on a particular concept or skill, an intervention for this student or that one, an enrichment activity for another, and so forth.

Start by looking for patterns in the data, specifically how many (what percentage of?) students demonstrate mastery vs. how many don't. Let this information lead you to decide whether, or how much, to re-teach or re-visit those concepts and skills. For instance, if the 7th grade teacher determines that 75% (3 out of 4) can't locate and label transition words, then he knows that he must insert re-teach-ing, or first-time teaching, into this process quickly. Conversely, if he decides that most students (85%) mastered the other parts of a paragraph, then he might schedule work on transition words for a later date, while intervening with those 15% students who need to catch up on the essential skills of recognizing the major parts of paragraphs.

Remember that there is no pat formula or one-size solution to instructional adjustments. You must draw on your experience and knowledge as well as the advice and practices of others, and *surely* your understanding of how *your* students learn and respond to instruction. Sometimes your adjustments will call for you to skip over a planned section of instruction or just to fine-tune a piece of it. Bigger adjustments might include re-structuring the lesson or a major subsection, or you may have to go clear back to teaching the pre-requisite skills that students should have learned in the previous grade or course.

Invite Students into the Process

One of the greatest gifts you can give to students is to increase their awareness of themselves as learners by inviting them into your process. Help them realize that you and they are working together and that they have enormous control over how well they progress.

Delivered as an admonition, however, such a concept will fall flat except upon those terrified by your delivery. Don't go there. Instead, think of this idea as a welcome message and an opportunity for each student to gain internal strengths—life skills, if you will—for meeting challenges and learning from them.

If you discuss your **formative assessment process** with your students—what you're doing, why you're doing it, and the kinds of information it gives you—you can invite students to perform their own formative assessments. Tell them this, or better yet, post something like this so that it stays in view:

> Every time you ask **why** about information you hear, or ask yourself **what** something means, or think about the **who, how**, or **where** of something you imagine, you are *learning how to learn*.

Create a climate of self-awareness in your classroom. Find ways of encouraging your students to self-analyze—to internalize data they receive including feedback from your formative assessments. Your goal over time is to help individual students recognize new tactics that work for them—tactics they can employ to facilitate their own learning—tactics that become habitual.

Here are a few examples of **learning tactics** that you can encourage students to employ:

Student Learning Tactics
USE LISTENING-TO-LEARN SKILLS: 1. **Listen specifically for foot-stompers**. For example, in a Jurisprudence Course, the professor introduced the Principles of Justice. One of the students tagged it as a foot stomper. She listened closely to what it was and noted where in the class textbook the Principals of Justice were described. She also made a mental note to reread that section of the book.

continued on next page

2. **Make pictures in your mind**. As the teacher presents enabling knowledge or teaches skills, visualize the organization of that knowledge in your mind.

3. **Pose questions to one self.** Ask yourself questions about what you don't fully understand: *Why is this important? Where have I seen something like this before?* Listen for places in the instruction that are not quite clear to you, turn that lack of clarity into a mental question, and listen to see if the teacher answers it as the lesson progresses.

4. **Think of examples of applying the knowledge.** For example, if a teacher is showing how to compute a math problem, mentally apply that process to another similar math problem, or even a more complex version.

5. **Make Connections.** Connect the new knowledge and skills with knowledge and skills you've previously learned.

USE PHYSICAL LEARNING TACTICS:

1. **Take notes**. Use some of the traditional ways to take notes, or…change it up a bit. Take notes on a graphic organizer, especially one tailored to the structure of the new knowledge.

2. **Sketch.** Capture important pieces of knowledge by making line drawings or cartoons, possibly with a one line caption underneath, or make sketches of things you envision or want to build.

3. **Focus Vocabulary.** Write the definitions of key vocabulary words so you can refer to them later. Again, you could illustrate the meaning and/or picture in your mind how you might act out the meaning of a word.

4. **Summarize.** At key junctures in the lesson, write a short summary of what you've learned.

NOTE: To examine formative assessment for multiple concepts and sub-skills, look at the Case Study that follows:

CASE STUDY

Formative Assessment for Multiple Concepts and Sub-Skills

Planning your formative assessment process for multiple concepts—e.g., those in a required standard—is a process that begins with studying the content of the requirement, unpacking the concepts and skills within, and focusing those concepts and skills in a learning progression that leads stepwise to student mastery of the intended learning outcome.

From such a planned progression, you can identify points or stages at which to assess students' learning, and you can create specific pre- and post-formative assessments to administer at the key points you determined so that you can organize and analyze the data from those assessments. Your plan—and the assessment devices you develop to gauge learning mastery—become (1) your road map through the concepts and skills within the standard, and (2) your contingency plans for adjusting your instruction along the way.[9]

See How Others Crafted a Multi-Concept Learning Progression

A team of fourth grade teachers tackled the following standard: Number and Operations in Base Ten. They began their collaborative work by recognizing the need for developing (1) a formal pre-formative assessment for each of their students to take at the outset of instruction, and (2) a post-formative assessment for each student after completion of first-time instruction. Specifically, the team agreed to do this:

1. Set a date by which each teacher will have administered, scored, and prepared the data display for collaborative analysis of pre-common formative assessment,

2. Block in the amount of time allocated to teaching the standard the first time, and

3. Set a date by which the post-assessment will be administered, scored and the data prepared for collaborative analysis.

In addition, the team decided to follow current research about the formative assessment process using an approach like the one recommended by W. James Popham, a nationally recognized expert on educational assessment. The team developed the following process as a series of steps:

Step 1: Identify and Study Content. Team members agreed that their best way of increasing student learning is to be clear themselves on the specifics of what students should know and be able to do. To gain clarity, the team analyzed the standard to penetrate the levels of specificity articulated within the objectives by identifying the concepts and skills therein.

Notice that the team began work by scrutinizing the skill requirements within the standard and by using graphic distinctions (italics and non-italics) to chunk its objectives:

Strand: NUMBER AND OPERATIONS IN BASE TEN (4.NBT)

Generalize place value understanding for multi-digit whole numbers by analyzing patterns, writing whole numbers in a variety of ways, making comparisons, and rounding (Standards 4.NBT.1–3). *Use place value understanding and properties of operations to perform multi-digit addition, subtraction, multiplication, and division using a one-digit divisor (Standards 4.NBT.4–6). Expectations in this strand are limited to whole numbers less than or equal to 1,000,000.*

Standard 4.NBT.1
Recognize that in a multi-digit whole number, a digit in one place represents ten times what it represents in the place to its right. For example, recognize that $700 \div 70 = 10$ by applying concepts of place value and division.

Standard 4.NBT.2
Read and write multi-digit whole numbers using base-ten numerals, number names, and expanded form. Compare two multi-digit numbers based on meanings of the digits in each place, using >, =, and < symbols to record the results of comparisons.

.

chart continues on next page

Standard 4.NBT.3
Use place value understanding to round multi-digit whole numbers to any place.

Standard 4.NBT.4
Fluently add and subtract multi-digit whole numbers using the standard algorithm.

Standard 4.NBT.5
Multiply a whole number of up to four digits by a one-digit whole number, and multiply two two-digit numbers, using strategies based on place value and the properties of operations. Illustrate and explain the calculation by using equations, rectangular arrays, and/or area models.

Standard 4.NBT.6
Find whole-number quotients and remainders with up to four-digit dividends and one-digit divisors, using strategies based on place value, the properties of operations, and/or the relationship between multiplication and division. Illustrate and explain the calculation by using equations, rectangular arrays, and/or area models.

The team was quick to recognize that this standard is fairly complex so chunking it into two parts (objectives 1-3 and 4-6) gave them logical points at which to administer assessment vehicles to gauge students' learning.

In addition, chunking the objectives within the standard led the team to closer scrutiny of the concepts and skills within each of those objectives.

Step 2: Develop a Learning Progression. The team looked closely at the concepts and skills within the standard's objectives #1-3 and kept their eyes on the learning outcome, which they agreed was this:

Learning Outcome (Objectives 1-3): *Generalize place value understanding for multi-digit whole numbers by analyzing patterns, writing whole numbers in a variety of ways, making comparisons, and rounding.*

Within those objectives, they were careful to recognize the concepts and skills as two distinct types, or categories: enabling knowledge and sub-skills. They understood that certain conceptual ideas or information (enabling knowledge) must precede the development of other skills (sub-skills), as the word "enabling" implies.

The team thought of a learning progression as a continuum of learning—one body of enabling knowledge that promotes the development of sub-skill(s), then another body of enabling knowledge that promotes additional sub-skills, and so on. NOTE: In the example that follows, these are numbered consecutively.

Once they assembled and grouped their enabling knowledge and sub-skills for objectives 1-3, the team outlined their learning progression into four groups, each containing a body of enabling knowledge and one or more sub-skills, and they estimated the number of lessons likely to reach their desired Learning Outcome:

Learning Progression (Objectives 1-3)
Leading to Learning Outcome for Standard 4.NBT

Learning Outcome 4.NBT, Objectives 1–3:

Generalize place value understanding for multi-digit whole numbers by analyzing patterns, writing whole numbers in a variety of ways, making comparisons, and rounding.

Body of Enabling Knowledge #1:

Recognize that in a multi-digit whole number, a digit in one place represents ten times what it represents in the place to its right. For example, recognize that $700 \div 70 = 10$ by applying concepts of place value and division.

Subskill #2: Apply concepts of place value and division or multiplication to mentally compute simple problems such as $10 \times 60 = 600$; or $600 / 60 = 10$

2 lessons

---

continued on next page

Body of Enabling Knowledge #3:
Multi-digit whole numbers can be read and written in three ways:
1. base-ten numerals,
2. number names, and
3. expanded form.

Subskill #4: Read and write multi-digit whole numbers using base-ten numerals.

Subskill #5: Read and write multi-digit whole numbers using number names.

Subskill #6: Read and write multi-digit whole numbers in expanded form.

5 lessons

Body of Enabling Knowledge #7: Two multi-digit numbers can be compared based on meanings of the digits in each place, using >, =, and < symbols to record the results of comparisons.

Subskill #8: Compare two multi-digit numbers based on meanings of the digits in each place, using >, <, = to record the results of the comparison.

2 lessons

Body of Enabling Knowledge #9: Use place value understanding to round multi-digit whole numbers to any place.

Subskill #10: Use place value understanding to round multi-digit whole numbers to a given place.

2 lessons

Step 3: Determine When to Elicit Assessment Data to Gauge Students' Learning. The complexity of the content (e.g., concepts and skills within the standard) as well as your learning progression itself can be instrumental in guiding your timing of formative assessments.

First, pay careful attention to the content: What are the discernable stages leading toward the learning outcome? Where are logical, conceptual breaks in the learning progression? The fourth grade team determined that the math standard 4.NBT contained two discernible stages, objectives 1-3 and 4-6, so they decided to administer pre- and post-formative assessments for each of those stages, or parts. On their plan, they called these stages Part I and Part II (model for Part I to follow).

The team's first pre-formative assessment (for Part I) would address each of the bodies of enabling knowledge as well as the associated sub-skills in their learning progression.

The math team agreed upon a planned sequence:

a. Administer the pre-assessment,
b. Organize the resulting data by student,
c. Collaboratively analyze the data, and
d. Plan differentiated first-time instruction that meets the needs of their students.

Step 4: Create the Pre-and Post-Formative Assessment.
Ready to prepare the specific items for their pre- and post-formative assessments, the team used their learning progression as the skeleton on which to hang their assessment items. Here is their body of Assessment Items for Part I, Standard 4.NBT, Objectives 1-3. Notice that the team developed four problems for each chunk of enabling knowledge (concept) and sub-skill:

Assessment Items   **Learning Progression Part I, Standard 4.NBT,**   **Objectives 1- 3**
Learning Outcome 4.NBT, Objectives 1– 3:   Generalize place value understanding for multi-digit whole numbers by analyzing patterns, writing whole numbers in a variety of ways, making comparisons, and rounding.

continued on next page

Body of Enabling Knowledge #1:

Recognize that in a multi-digit whole number, a digit in one place represents ten times what it represents in the place to its right. For example, recognize that $700 \div 70 = 10$ by applying concepts of place value and division.

In the space on the left of each item, write the letter that shows the correct answer to the problem.

_____1. 80 x 60 =   _____3. 700 x 90 =

      (a.) 480   (c.) 4,800   (a.) 6,300   (c.) 63

      (b.) 48   (d.) 486   (b.) 630   (d.) 63,000

_____2. 800/40 =   _____4. 700/10

      (a.) 20   (c.) 2   (a.) 70   (c.) 700

      (b.) 200   (d.) 2,000   (b.) 7,000   (d.) 7

Subskill #2: Apply concepts of place value and division or multiplication to mentally compute simple problems such as $10 \times 60 = 600$; or $600 / 60 = 10$

1. 800/80 = _____   3. 9,000/30 = _____

2. 800 x 80 = _____   4. 70 x 600 = _____

2 lessons

Body of Enabling Knowledge #3:

Multi-digit whole numbers can be read and written in three ways:
1. base-ten numerals,
2. number names, and
3. expanded form.

In the space on the left of each item, put a T if the number sentence is true or false if it is incorrect.

_____1. 8 x 10,000 + 9 x 100 + 3 x 10 + 6 x 1 = 80,936

_____2. 7 x 1,000, 6x 100, 9 x 1 = 7,609

_____3. 81,009 = eighty-one thousand nine

_____4. six thousand seventy-one = 671

continued on next page

Subskill #4: Read and write multi-digit whole numbers using base-ten numerals.

For each item below, write the following multi-digit whole numbers using base-ten numerals in space provided.

1. During May, Jack rode his bicycle for five hundred thirty-five miles. _____

2. Jody talked on the telephone for one hundred twenty-three minutes. _____

3. One hundred fifty-one thousand, four hundred sixty-nine

_____

4. Five thousand seventeen _____

Subskill #5: Read and write multi-digit whole numbers using number names.

Write each of the numbers below using number names in the space provided on the right.

1. 987 _____

2. 5,000,067 _____

3. 18,598_____

4. 9,003 _____

5. 14,011 _____

Subskill #6: Read and write multi-digit whole numbers in expanded form.

Write the following numbers in expanded form:

   1. 8,009   2. 6,718   3. 7,670   4. 78,009

5 lessons

continued on next page

Body of Enabling Knowledge #:7 Two multi-digit numbers can be compared based on meanings of the digits in each place, using >, =, and < symbols to record the results of comparisons.

In the space on the left of each number sentence, place a T if it is True and an F if it is False.

_____1. 101,010 > 101, 010   _____3. 207,600 = 207,600

_____2. 157,072 < 175,072   _____4. 1,897,401 > 1,897,479

Subskill #8: Compare two multi-digit numbers based on meanings of the digits in each place, using >, <, = to record the results of the comparison.

Write the symbol >, <, or = in the blank that correctly compares the two numbers:

1. 9,890 _____9,980   3. 70,809 _____70,819

2. 42,068 _____42,058   4. 380,437 _____ 390,437

2 lessons

Body of Enabling Knowledge #9: Use place value understanding to round multi-digit whole numbers to any place.

Select the letter that correctly shows the numbers rounded to the given place. Write the answer in the space provided on the left.

_____1. Round 4,051 to the nearest 100s.
    (a.) 4,501   (c.) 5,000
    (b.) 4,100   (d.) 4,160

_____2. Round 409,082 to the nearest 10,000s.
    (a.) 400,900   (c.) 410,000
    (b.) 490,000   (d.) 500,000

_____3. Round 8,424 to the nearest 1000s.
    (a.) 8,000   (c.) 8,500
    (b.) 9,000   (d.) 9,400

_____4. Round 2,678,128 to the nearest 100,000s.
    (a.) 2,680,000   (c.) 2,700,000
    (b.) 3,000,000   (d.) 2,678,100

continued on next page

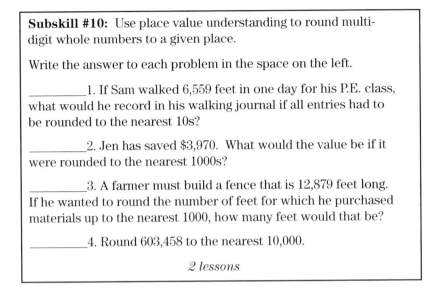

Subskill #10: Use place value understanding to round multi-digit whole numbers to a given place.

Write the answer to each problem in the space on the left.

_____1. If Sam walked 6,559 feet in one day for his P.E. class, what would he record in his walking journal if all entries had to be rounded to the nearest 10s?

_____2. Jen has saved $3,970. What would the value be if it were rounded to the nearest 1000s?

_____3. A farmer must build a fence that is 12,879 feet long. If he wanted to round the number of feet for which he purchased materials up to the nearest 1000, how many feet would that be?

_____4. Round 603,458 to the nearest 10,000.

2 lessons

Step 5. Administer the Pre-Common Formative Assessment (CFA). The team administered their pre-common formative assessment to all students taught by the team and made additional decisions about it: (1) they decided to grade each student's test with the assessment in hand so that they could discern which specific aspects of place value each student might struggle with, (2) they decided to score each assessment item as follows:

<u>Mastery</u> = answered all four problems correctly.

<u>Approaching Mastery</u> = answered three out of four problems correctly.

<u>Below Mastery</u> = answered two or fewer problems correctly.

and, (3) they decided to develop a post-CFA that mirrored their pre-CFA.

Step 6. Organize the Data for each Student by Chunks of Enabling Knowledge and Sub-skill. The team organized the scores from the pre-CFA in order to show the data by student—specifically, how each student scored on each chunk of enabling knowledge and sub-skill. They did this to plan first-time instruction strategically, thereby increasing the number of students likely to achieve mastery.

Here is an example showing how one of the teachers assembled data for the Body of Enabling Knowledge #3 and its related sub-skills: #4, #5, #6. This teacher organized students' names in an ascending order of mastery to help identify patterns and also graphically distinguished the score levels as follows:

Data for Body of Enabling Knowledge #3 and its Related Sub-skills: #4, #5, #6						
Students	Preceding chunks of Enabling Knowledge, sub-skills.	Enabling Knowledge #3 Multi-digit whole numbers can be...	Subskill #4. Read and write ... base ten numerals.	Subskill #5: Read and write ... using number names.	Subskill #6: Read and write ... in expanded form.	Subsequent Enabling Knowledge and Skills.
Joe		Below	Below	Below	Below	
Serena		Below	Below	Below	Below	
Maria		Below	Approach	Below	Below	
Gunther		Below	Approach	Below	Below	
Kjerston		Approach	Approach	Below	Below	
David		Approach	Approach	Below	Below	
Soren		Approach	Approach	Below	Below	
Tawny		Approach	Approach	Approach	Below	
Kim		Approach	Approach	Approach	Approach	
Raphael		Approach	Approach	Approach	Approach	
Bolin		Mastery	Mastery	Mastery	Mastery	
Andrea		Mastery	Mastery	Mastery	Mastery	

The graphic coding helps patterns pop out so that the team is positioned to analyze the data collaboratively and to use that information to plan first-time instruction strategically.

The team learned about research by school improvement expert Bambric-Sontoya, who recommends analyzing the data first at the enabling knowledge/sub-skills level and then at the student level. The team began this work by matching findings with actions that they could take.

The next example shows the Sontoya recommendation in the first column regarding Levels of Analysis, Findings in the second column that represent the basis for differentiating first-time instruction, and in the third column the Actions that teachers can take.

Analysis of Data for Body of Enabling Knowledge and Related Sub-skills		
Level of Analysis	**Findings**	**Actions**
Enabling Knowledge/Skills	1. All but 4 students are either approaching or have mastered enabling knowledge #3. 2. 10 of 12 students are approaching or at mastery. 3. For Subskills #5 and #6, 10 of 12 students are approaching or below mastery. For both subskills, at least seven scored below mastery.	1. Give a quick review of Read and Write Multi-Digit Whole Numbers Using Base 10 Numerals. Do a quick formative assessment. Allow students who are ready to do independent practice. Reteach those not ready in small group. 2. Use same strategy as above. 3. Spend most of allotted time teaching and reteaching Subskills #5 and #6

continued on next page

Student Level	1. Joe, Serena, Maria, and Gunther are below grade level on at least three out of four of the Knowledge or sub-skills. 2. Bolin and Andrea have mastered all four areas.	1. Pre-teach Joe, Serena, Maria, and Gunther each enabling knowledge and subskill prior to teaching to whole class. Provide small group instruction while rest of class works independently. 2. Provide Bolin and Andrea instruction at the next level of learning for place value (5th grade). Provide independent practice at that level.

Note: This data analysis is merely a snippet of a data display for the pre-CFA for this standard. A complete data analysis would display assessment results for all chunks of enabling knowledge and sub-skills in the Learning Progression for Objectives 1-3.

Step 7. Administer and Analyze the Post-Common Formative Assessment (CFA). The team's post-CFA formative assessment mirrored the pre-CFA, and team members applied similar procedures for scoring, organizing and displaying data, and analyzing.

The main difference at the post-CFA stage is this: Post-CFA data and analysis leads to specific interventions for students who have not mastered particular chunks of enabling knowledge and sub-skills, and to enrichment for students who have demonstrated mastery for most or all chunks of enabling knowledge and sub-skills.

Consult Experts

1. Ainsworth, L. and Viegut, D. *Common Formative Assessments: How to Connect Standards-based Instruction and Assessment.* Thousand Oaks, CA: Corwin Press, 2006.

2. Bambrick-Santoyo, P. *Driven by Data: A Practical Guide to Improve Instruction.* San Francisco, CA: Jossey-Bass, 2010.

3. Black, P. J. and Wiliam, D. "Assessment and Classroom Learning." *Principles, Policy & Practice* 5 (1) 1998.

4. Crooks, T. J. "The Impact of Classroom Evaluation Practices on Students." *Review of Educational Research* 58 (4) 1988.

5. Fuchs, L. S. and Fuchs, D. "Effects of Systematic Formative Evaluation – A Meta-Analysis." *Exceptional Children* 53 (3) 1986.

6. Gareis, C. R. and Grant, L. W. *Teacher-Made Assessments: How to Connect Curriculum, Instruction, and Student Learning.* Larchmont, NY: Eye on Education, 2008.

7. Himmele, P. and Himmele, W. *Total Participation Techniques: Making Every Student an Active Learner.* Alexandria, VA: ASCD, 2011.

8. Natriello, G. "The Impact of Evaluation Processes on Students." *Educational Psychologist* 2(2) 1987.

9. Popham, W. J. *Transformative Assessment.* Alexandria, VA: ASCD, 2008.

10. Wiliam, D. *Embedded Formative Assessment.* Bloomington, IN: Solution Tree Press, 2011.

Self Assess:
Formative Assessment in a Single Lesson

For each element, self-assess using the following 1-4 scale:

1. Missing (I need to do this)
2. Attempted (I try to do this, but I am not successful)
3. Apparent (I do this well, but I don't do it consistently. When I do it, it works!)
4. Well Done (I do this consistently and appropriately)

Planning   1   2   3   4
My formative assessment process is planned.

Learning Outcome   1   2   3   4
I identify an intended learning outcome for each lesson.

Learning Progression   1   2   3   4
I create a learning progression for each lesson that is
comprised of measurable chunks of enabling knowledge and sub-skills
that students must grasp as they progress toward mastering
the intended learning outcome.

Assessment Vehicles   1   2   3   4
I create and administer questions, quizzes, or all-respond
tasks that specifically measure the blocks of enabling
knowledge or sub-skills as each are addressed in the lesson.

Instructional Adjustments   1   2   3   4
I use the assessment-elicited data to make instructional
adjustments that usually involve giving more instruction
(re-teaching, showing more examples, etc.) or moving
forward to the next block of knowledge or sub-skill.

Communication   1   2   3   4
At lesson start, I post and present the intended learning
outcome to students and communicate how mastering
this knowledge and related skills will help in their
current and future lives.

Look-Fors   1   2   3   4
I also present the success criteria derived from the
learning progression that gives students things to look for
to monitor their progress toward mastery of the intended
learning outcome.

Sharing Data   1   2   3   4
I share formative assessment data with students as it is
collected and help them reflect on and adjust their
learning tactics when needed.

Students' Tools for Learning   1   2   3   4
I explicitly teach and model a variety of learning tactics
to students and facilitate opportunities for students to reflect on their
learning tactics and adjust when needed.

Self-Assess:
Formative Assessment across Multiple Lessons

For each element, self-assess using the following 1-4 scale:

1. **Missing (I need to do this)**
2. **Attempted (I try to do this, but I am not successful)**
3. **Apparent (I do this well, but I don't do it consistently. When I do it, it works!)**
4. **Well Done (I do this consistently and appropriately)**

Planning   1   2   3   4
My formative assessment process is planned.

Learning Progression   1   2   3   4
I/we create a learning progression for concepts and skills within the
standard or multiple lessons.

Using Pre-Common Formative Assessment   1   2   3   4
I/we use the learning progression to create a pre-common formative
assessment (CFA) for each standard.

Administering the Pre-CFA   1   2   3   4
I/we administer the pre-CFA to students before beginning first-time
teaching of the standard or multiple lessons.

Displaying Data   1   2   3   4
I/we display data from the pre-CFA in a table by student, by concept,
by skill, and by sub-skill.

Analyzing Data   1   2   3   4
I /we analyze pre-CFA data at both the concept and skill levels.

Planning Instructional Adjustments   1   2   3   4
I/we record our findings from the analysis of pre-CFA data and then
determine and make notes of instructional actions for each.

Planning First-Time Instruction   1   2   3   4
I/we use the information for the analysis of the data to plan
differentiated first-time instruction.

Delivering Differentiated Instruction   1   2   3   4
I/we deliver planned differentiated instruction the first time
we teach the enabling knowledge and sub-skills of the
multiple lessons or focused standard.

Collaborating   1   2   3   4
I collaborate with my team to plan and implement the process for
each standard we teach.

Global Positioning Systems (GPSs) collect and process feedback about your progress in order to guide you along your course while recalculating your direction as necessary.

CHAPTER
FIVE

Facilitate Feedback That Ensures Growth

two-way communication ... self-assessment ... feedback

By mid-year, all teachers in Viola Lacey's school had worked to meet their principal's goal: to develop methods for meeting the individual needs of all students across all ages, diverse backgrounds, and varying abilities. From the outset, Viola's general strategy had been two-fold: to pace valuable research and information across the year's professional development days, and to ensure that those meetings contain transferable tactics and methods for her teachers. And—very important to Viola!—she sketched follow-up opportunities for her teachers to synthesize what they learn and to share and devise together in ways that will affect their lesson planning.

Deepen Your Communication with Students

By this point, mentor Clay Briggs had worked with everyone in Mary Pat's interdisciplinary team, and so the team invited him to one of their meetings devoted to continuing their work on formative assessment. Specifically, the team was looking for ways to strengthen their instructional techniques as they put their formative assessment data in play during lessons. Clay began the meeting this way:

"Imagine this," he said. "You are a 7th grade teacher. You have given your class an assignment to write argumentation like you did, Dan, earlier in the year. As each student makes a list of ideas to support his or her central thesis (the argument), you monitor the work. You especially like the way Yana is dividing her ideas into two columns (pros and cons) so you say 'Great work, Yana!' She smiles at your kind feedback as you move on to the next desk.

"Now, RATE the value of your feedback by choosing a number along this scale:

Worthless   0   1   2   3   4   5   Invaluable"

The team paused. A tentative "3?" from Marge made the group giggle. "Easy fence-straddle, Marge," Clay said.

"Well, if you decided the feedback value is near zero, many researchers would agree with you. Yana learned virtually nothing about her work from your feedback (other than your approval, which is not entirely worthless). But imagine if you had said 'Yana, your groupings of pros and cons show that you have a keen sense for distinguishing differences, the differing sides of an argument.' Feedback like that—information that allows your student to recognize her strengths—encourages her to call upon those strengths in future situations next week, next year, and on and on. And, Dan, your feedback may very well help her when you teach compare and contrast next semester!"

THE TEAM AGREED: Beware the siren song of high praise, the weakest form of feedback, a dead end because it offers no tangible information. Instead, root your praise in ideas that will grow, and fertilize it with details.

Why Does Anybody Need Feedback?

Feedback is part of life. From infancy to old age, each of us gets messages from others. Feedback in classroom situations is part of that learning continuum, so many talented educators have made important observations from careful study of the impact of feedback on the learning process in classroom situations. For instance, Hattie's meta-analysis of 138 influences on learning revealed that feedback was in the top five to ten; that is, feedback is more influential than 128 other key influences on learning. [3,4]

Hattie & Timberly view feedback as important information that results directly from performance.[1] The internationally respected researcher Wiliam adds that feedback must be couched relative to a desired outcome.[13] All agree that feedback impacts learning in positive ways when it communicates information relative to a goal which causes the learner to modify his or her thinking or behavior. Put another way, feedback enhances learning if it contains information on aspects of performance (related to a desired outcome, of course) that encourages the learner to modify his or her thinking and behavior in progressing toward the goal. Understanding what feedback is is one thing; developing and delivering feedback correctly is the next step, and it becomes the crux of the matter for every teacher.

Deliver Feedback Effectively

Make the content within your feedback descriptive and constructive so that it is meaningful to your student, and make your feedback clearly relevant to the work at hand. And be mindful of the long arm of your feedback because its value isn't just a measure of what's happening now; it's a way of engaging your student in thinking about his or her actions going forward. Consider this process from the work of Dylan Wiliam:

Feedback Delivery Methods

FOCUS Your Feedback. Whether your feedback is spoken or written, narrow it to only a few key aspects so that it does not appear daunting. Keep it focused on performance aspects that s/he can modify or utilize for future success.

FRAME Your Feedback. Put your comments into the context of the lesson objectives, knowledge, or skills. It helps if you have presented these at the outset of the lesson and if you post them as well. Feedback is especially useful if you associate it with the desired outcome.

Provoke FORWARD Motion. Allow feedback to encourage your student to think about future performance, consciously or by implication. If possible, provide time or opportunity for your student to modify an action or replicate learning in a new context.[13]

Keep a Feedback Process in Mind: **FOCUS FRAME FORWARD**

Create and Manage Feedback with Clarity

First map the segments of the learning (e.g., lesson parts, sub-skills) and present the criteria for success. Then craft feedback in terms of those aspects. And as you deliver feedback, stay attuned to your student's responsiveness. Here are three key management challenges you face as you think about, plan, and deliver instruction along with feedback and formative assessment:

1. Help Your Student Answer *Where am I going?*

Plan ahead for the signposts your student will look for, the mile markers along the way—in short, map the journey so that you can craft feedback for each of those steps. In effect, the feedback you give is your communication system, which (1) clarifies the status at each leg of the learning journey, and (2) keeps the final destination in sight.[10, 13]

Frey and Frey call this **Feeding Up**, letting students know at the outset of the learning journey what the destination is and the markers to look for in order to know they are progressing toward the destination. In the Feed Up phase of feedback, the goal (objective or learning target) clarifies the full outcome while the success criteria breaks it down into smaller units of knowledge and skills that you and your students can use to monitor their progress toward attaining the desired outcome.[6]

Here's an example from a fourth grade teacher's plan for students to learn the water cycle. Since the larger goal is for students to demonstrate that they understand the water cycle, you create a success criteria by breaking down that goal into smaller units of knowledge and sub-skills that students must master as they progress toward achieving the full goal over a series of lessons:

Desired Outcome for Multiple Lessons: *I can show that water changes state as it moves through the water cycle by drawing and explaining it from memory and applying that knowledge to real world situations.*

Criteria for Success: *I will know I can do this when I can...*

  a. locate examples of evaporation and condensation in the water cycle.
  b. describe the process of evaporation, condensation, and precipitation as they relate to the water cycle.
  c. identify locations that hold water as it passes through the water cycle (e.g., oceans, atmosphere, fresh surface water, snow, ice, and ground water).
  d. construct a model or diagram to show how water continuously moves through the water cycle over time.
  e. describe how the water cycle relates to the water supply in my community.

Sadler found that communicating to students up front what they will be learning clarifies and accomplishes many things.[9] First, when students fully understand where they are going, they are more motivated to get there. Second, when the desired outcome is broken down into smaller units of knowledge and sub-skills (success criteria), students feel more confident in their developing ability to get there; thus, they are more likely to engage. Third, communicating a success criterion gives both you and each student mile markers by which to monitor progress toward achieving the outcome. You can give formative assessments at each unit of knowledge/sub-skill, and students can use the feedback you give them to improve their performance by adjusting their thinking, their actions, and their learning tactics (e.g., listen more carefully, take more detailed notes, mentally rehearse new knowledge/skills, make diagrams that capture the information, and so forth).

2. Help Your Student Understand *How am I going?*

This is where rubber meets the road in the process of providing feedback. Feedback that answers *How am I going?* provides students with tightly-focused information about their progress relative to the desired outcome. It indicates the aspects of the attempt that were accurate and/or inaccurate. This feedback includes a pathway forward by providing insights into actions learners can take or activities in which they can engage to advance toward mastery.[10, 13]

Here's an example:

Feedback Example: *How am I going?*

A high school physical education teacher taught weight lifting. At the outset of the lesson, he articulated the desired outcome and gave success criteria for the correct body position for lifting. He taught and modeled the lifting positions emphasizing key aspects and then engaged students in practicing that lifting position.

While students lifted weights, he assessed and gave each student focused feedback that included aspects of their posi-

continued on next page

tions that were correct and a few aspects that needed to be modified with suggestions for how to improve. As a result of his feedback, students knew what they did well, areas they needed to adjust, and a strategy for how to improve their lifting position.

3. Point Your Student to *Where next?*

Your feedback can help students move forward in specific ways by (a) focusing on aspects of their initial attempt they'd like to strengthen or expand, and (b) gaining clearer focus for the next challenge to take on. *Next* feedback helps prepare students to self-regulate their learning by promoting deeper understanding, greater fluency/automaticity, additional strategies and processes to work on tasks, and still more self-regulation.[10,13] Here's a simple example:

Feedback Example: *Where next?*

An art student produced a portrait according to **success criteria** that included seven elements. The teacher gave him specific feedback on each of the seven criteria to show him which elements he met successfully and which needed modification.

The student and teacher celebrated those successes, and the student selected two of the seven criteria that he determined to improve:

Criterion #2: *I will create movement, or flow of figures, to guide viewers through the scene.*

Criterion #6: *I will draw figures and objects in appropriate proportions.*

The student focused on these two criteria as he prepared sketches for his next portrait, paying close attention to movement and proportionality as he planned forward.

Target Levels of Feedback

Research offers significant insight into four different types, or levels, of feedback that you can offer students.

Four Levels of Feedback
Task Level: Information relative to a student's attempts to master a learning outcome. **Process Level:** Information about a student's process in completing tasks or creating product. **Self-Regulation Level:** Information that makes a student aware of what they (a) know, (b) can achieve, or (c) have learned. **Self Level:** Generalized praise without specific information or descriptive detail.[3]

Most frequently, teachers rely on task-level feedback, which can be viable and valuable. Many teachers offer self-level feedback, which isn't very useful, albeit supportive. Feedback on the process level and the self-regulation level, on the other hand, offer possibilities for you to strengthen your feedback and to facilitate student learning in very significant ways.

1. *Task-Level* Feedback.

This kind of feedback is particularly valuable when students are learning something new or for students who struggle with mastery overall. Task-level feedback isn't as general as self-feedback because it focuses on a specific task—for instance, if you confirm for a student that s/he is correct or not correct about something. Your written comments that offer insight into the student's performance or product—those are task-level feedback. (But grades are not feedback, per se; they are assessment.)

Black and Wiliam suggest two main functions of feedback, *Directive and Facilitative*, each of which serves a purpose. Directive communicates exactly what needs to be corrected or revised. Facilitative provides guidance and suggestions that help students revise and re-conceptualize.[1]

Offering Directive and Facilitative Feedback

Learning Target: *I can write the <u>topic sentence</u> of an argumentation paper.*

Success Criteria: This means my sentence will:
- introduce the topic,
- state my position, and
- state my position in an arguable way that invokes strong agreement or disagreement.

Student's first attempt: *Scientists have shown that global warming is real.*

Directive Feedback might be expressed this way:
You've stated this as a fact. You need to revise it to be argumentative: cause the reader to agree or disagree.

Facilitative Feedback might be presented this way:
Remember your first statement should be stated in an arguable way that provokes a strong cognitive and emotional response of agreement or disagreement. How might you revise this sentence to achieve that response?

Facilitative Feedback requires a bit of strategic planning. An example shared by Wiliam is a feedback strategy that an English teacher has used: *The Three Question Strategy.* As she reads each student's writing, she looks for three aspects that need to be improved. Beside each area, the teacher writes a number (1, 2, or 3) that correlates with one of three questions that she places at the end of the paper. Each question invites the student to reflect on how s/he might revise that area to more effectively meet the goals articulated in the Learning Outcome and Success Criteria, such as: *1. How might you use other literary devices to reveal the character more fully to the reader, such as character's thoughts, flashbacks into past life, reaction to events, and so forth? 2. How might you introduce more suspense into the story? 3. How can you further develop the events that led to the solution of the problem?* Each student revises those areas of the paper and resubmits it.

Scaffolded Feedback can take you still further into your students' formative growth experience. Researcher Ian Smith suggests scaffolding feedback by creating a feedback grid. For instance, you might develop the Criteria for Success yourself or with your students' input, and then place it on a grid on which you quickly indicate your feedback. Here's an example from an assignment about making a map to show the route of Lewis and Clarke's Expedition. Notice that it outlines 6 criteria for success and 3 types of feedback.

Outcome: A map showing the route of Lewis and Clarke's expeditions with annotations of four or more crucial events along the route. **Criteria for Success**	Feedback: + = Meets Criteria ? = Incomplete x = Missing/ incorrect
1. The map includes each leg of Lewis and Clarke's expedition.	+
2. Each leg is shown correctly, relative to the geographical area.	+
3. The map legend shows symbols for each type of information represented.	?

continued on next page

4. Each important region or settlement is labeled correctly on the map.	x
5. Key Topographical features are placed and labeled correctly.	+
6. Four crucial events are marked at the place they occurred and are companied by short explanatory paragraphs.	?

Scaffolded Feedback does not take long to prepare and helps students to see exactly which criteria they've met and which they need to improve. Because students see the task outlined before them, they are likely to see it as doable and therefore become more likely to engage in making revisions.

Feedback at the task level helps students improve their performance on a particular task, but usually it is not transferrable. If you wish to help students transfer what they learn from one specific task to others, then treat feedback at the task level as a staging area from which you can develop new and additional feedback at the process and self-regulation levels.

2. *Process-Level* Feedback.

Your process-level feedback focuses on the ways in which a student approaches the task—the process s/he uses to master a skill, solve a problem, gain information, create a product, etc. Your purpose is to develop your student's processes still further so that s/he can build upon them, sharpen them, and apply them in different ways as s/he tackles new or subsequent tasks. Here's an example:

Example of Process-Level Feedback

A seventh grade teacher instructed students to use close reading techniques to understand and respond to informational text and listed several techniques for them to consider:

- highlighting key facts such as people, dates, etc.
- using brackets around key ideas and important passages.
- looking up unfamiliar terms and writing synonyms in the margin.

As students worked, the teacher interacted with individuals and then with the whole group to reflect on how they used the techniques. Specifically, they discussed the techniques they found most helpful, they considered additional techniques suggested by some students, and then they applied those processes to the next selection.

In addition, the teacher engaged students in reflecting on the effectiveness of these techniques by using strategies like these:

1. With your elbow partner, discuss how each of these techniques helped you comprehend the informational text and use the information to write a full explanation of this scientific phenomenon.

2. Brainstorm with your group about different places and situations in which you could use these close reading techniques. Record your ideas on chart paper at your table.

You can deliver process-level feedback one-on-one, in groups, or with an entire class. In any of these feedback situations, your key is the reflection part—the coaching you provide to elicit students' understanding of the value of a certain process, how it worked this time, and how it can be of use next time with even greater success.

Here is another example that you can find on the Teaching Channel about an intermediate grade math teacher who helps her students use an analytic process to detect and correct errors.

Example of Process-Level Feedback

Each morning students solve a strategically-selected math problem on a 3 by 5 card with no name attached. The teacher collects and sorts the cards into "no" (incorrect) and "yes" (correct) piles. First, she selects and projects a card from the "no" pile and directs students to use this process to detect and correct the error:

1. Find all the parts that were done correctly.
2. Identify where the first mistake was made.
3. Trace how that mistake rippled throughout the rest of the problem.
4. Rework the problem correctly.[8]

Together as a class, students identify what was done correctly, where the first mistake was made, and then they solve the problem correctly.

This daily exercise gives students immediate feedback on the problem they worked (task level), helps them use a strategy (process) to detect and correct errors, and views student-mistakes as a healthy part of learning. This process helps students develop a perception of learning ability as incremental, rather than fixed, and encourages increasing one's abilities by strategically using processes to identify and correct mistakes.

In most cases, and especially when working with a group or entire class, your process-level feedback will be facilitative. You will act like a coach as you elicit students' perceptions about their performance with the processes and techniques they are using. Your goal with process-level feedback is two-fold: (1) to build students concepts about their own abilities as they pertain to performance now and in the future, and (2) to move students into the self-regulatory level.

Still another way to give process-level feedback is by explicitly teaching students several learning tactics (take notes, ask question in head, mentally rehearse new information or skill, draw sketches, listen carefully for footstompers, and so forth). Then have them reflect and decide which type of learning situation each tactic might be most useful for.

Here is another example from Connie Toone, a mathematics coach in Brigham City, Utah, who uses a "Reciprocal Teaching Process" to help students understand and solve story problems in math:

Example of Reciprocal Teaching (Process-Level Feedback)

Today's Math Story Problem

1. Read the problem twice, using close reading techniques …
   a. the first time to identify and underline the key question,
   b. the second time to highlight important relevant information, circle words you don't understand, and to look for and write down the hidden question (which usually signals that it is a two-step problem).

2. Make a visual representation of the problem and solution.

3. Write an equation with the correct answer.

4. Reflect on the steps you took to solve the problem.

… and the Results

Student Janelle Wilson wrote this:

1. *I read the story problem two times.*
2. *The first time I found and underlined the question.*
3. *The second time, I highlighted important information.*
4. *I drew a picture of the story problem showing the solution.*
5. *I wrote the equation with the answer.*
6. *I wrote down the steps I took to solve the problem.*

Jannelle's answers are good descriptions of what she did, but Connie engaged in dialogue to facilitate deeper reflection. Specifically, in her answers to step 3, Jannelle had looked only for important pieces of information but not for the hidden questions or words she didn't understand. Jannelle had initially solved the problem incorrectly, but through process-level feedback, she and Connie recognized that the story problem required two steps to solve it successfully.

> **Note to Self:** Engage in a dialogue with the individual student or whole class to help discover other critical things they did or did not do to arrive at a correct answer. Focus on the thinking processes students used to develop and/or modify the visual representation they drew of the problem, and how they solved glitches or steps they missed that could have led to the correct solution.

It bears repeating that student reflection—process-level feedback and reciprocal teaching—leads students to deeper understandings that go way beyond the current task or problem. Reflection helps every student understand and enhance their learning processes. In the example of math story problems, student reflections strengthen their facility with story problems in current and future situations, and reflection helps students develop a deeper understanding of important practices that mathematicians use in their work every day.

3. *Self-Regulation* Feedback.

Ideally, this kind of feed-back expands upon the work of process-level feedback. It invites learners to own their learning and to use their self-awareness to apply and/or adjust (self regulate) their performance in future learning situations.

Self-regulation feedback helps to build a student's conscious knowledge about what s/he knows, can do, and has learned from experience. Research tells us that a self-regulating student can marshal his or her cognitive and emotional resources and take action that enhances future learning. According to Wiliam, the premise of self-assessment is that students can gain insight into their own learning to improve it.[13] Wiliam and Black believe that students are honest about their self-assessment; they are just as likely to judge their work too harshly as too kindly.[1] However, if students have a clear picture of what the desired learning outcome is and what the criteria for success is, they can reflect forward to manage their learning (*Where am I going?*), reflect back to refine their learning (*How am I going?*), and discern where to go next (*Where to next?*). In other words, they are processing sequenced levels of information (including feedback that you tailor for them) so that they can tailor their current and future actions.

Use Feedback To Help Students Self-Assess

To go full bore on making feedback useful for your students, craft opportunities for them to self-assess—that is, to create their own feedback. Use the following example of a Learning Outcome to follow a series of possibilities for self assessment.

> **Learning Outcome:** *I can introduce a claim and support it persuasively.*
> ### Success Criteria
> 1. I can write a thesis statement that makes a precise, provable claim.
> 2. In my introduction, I can distinguish my claim from counter-claims.
> 3. I can develop and organize evidence and reasons to support my claim while presenting and clarifying arguments against counter-claims.

1. **Self-Assess:** *Where am I going?*

Once students clearly understand the intended learning objective, or outcome, provide them with an opportunity to assess the success criteria by posing questions like these:

- Which parts of the success criteria do I already understand?
- Which part do I least understand?

- What learning tactic might I use to understand and be able to do it properly?

- What problems might I have in presenting a claim in a persuasive way? Distinguishing my claim from counter-claims? Developing and organizing evidence and reasons?

- What steps can I take to avoid these problems?

2. Self-Assess: *How am I going?*

You can develop a rubric for students to apply to their self-assessments of each success criterion. Have them do this once their work is underway because you will ask them to dip into their performance to show examples, or evidence, from their work to support their self-assessment. Here's an example of a form you can use for this kind of self data collection:

Success Criteria	My Rating Low High	Evidence from My Work
To what degree did I make a precise claim?	1 2 3	
How well have I distinguished my claim from counter-claims?	1 2 3	
How well have I developed and organized evidence and reasons to support my claim?	1 2 3	
How effectively have I organized and clarified my arguments against counter claims?	1 2 3	

A strength of this approach is to help your student look at his or her work in nuanced ways, viewing the work not as right or wrong, but as a work in progress, thus engendering a view of ability as incremental, something in reach, something that s/he can shape.

3. Self-Assess: *Where to Next?*

Once you think that students are ready to progress beyond meeting the success criteria, you can encourage them to take stock of the work they've done. The strength of this kind of self assessment is that it builds on the current success (they are "getting it" and completing the criteria with competency) by judging the work with an eye toward making it better still.   But this kind of self assessment doesn't just help the student up his work from a B to a B+ or from a B+ to an A, it lays the ground work for strengthening competency in future endeavors that will call upon these and similar skills.

Here's another way to look at it: You are making your student a co-owner of the learning while building confidence along the way. You can do this by having your student answer questions like these:

- Which parts of my introduction were the strongest?
- Which parts do I need to strengthen or refine?
- On which one or two parts will I focus my effort?
- What steps can I take to strengthen those parts?

Your most desired result—the reason you scaffold your feedback through these stages—is your student's state of mind in which s/he can see a relationship between effort and results which builds a sense of self efficacy—a most essential element of continued learning.

Use "Self Feedback" Cautiously

The fourth type of feedback, **Self-Level Feedback**, is something that probably every teacher has used (*"Gamma, that's great work!"*) but often the teacher misses an opportunity to offer task- or process-level feedback, which could be more useful to the student.

Seldom does self-level feedback translate into greater commitment, motivation, self-efficacy, or self-regulatory behavior. It is more likely to promote a student's sense that ability is fixed and there is not much anyone can do about it.

Education experts like Grant Wiggins offer at least two ways to break the habit of giving generalized praise by adding specific actionable information into the feedback.

Self-Feedback Enrichment Methods

Approach #1: Follow a general praise statement with details that help the learner see what s/he did well and how to sustain it or make it even better.

<u>General Praise</u>

1. You're a very good writer.

2. Great work, Anne.

<u>With Actionable Information Added</u>

1. You're a very good writer because your use of descriptive details makes the reader understand your idea clearly.

2. Great work, Anne. Here again you choose good facts and then organize them effectively.

Approach #2: Drop the praise statement and simply give the specific information about the task.

The way you know how to differentiate useful from non-useful information and predict which operations to use will help you solve problems you meet in the future.

Your attention to detail on each stage of the water cycle makes your diagram especially informative, which is a skill you can use when you create other products.

Position Students To Receive and Utilize Feedback Constructively

Teachers play a crucial role in creating the conditions in which students develop into self-regulating learners. As you work on inculcating student self-reflection through various levels of feedback, remain focused on the big picture. That is, seek always to broaden students' receptivity while leading students toward applying their self-knowledge to present and future tasks.

Help students develop a learning orientation. Too often, when confronted with a failure or when encountering challenging learning situations, some students tend to withdraw. The problem that they face is not seeing or understanding the relationship between their own efforts and what they can accomplish. You can help solve such a problem.

The work of researchers like Shute and Wiliam make it clear that students' own senses of their abilities and intelligences greatly influences how they learn—and how successfully they operate as learners. Help your students perceive ability or intelligence as innate conditions so that they take a performance orientation toward learning and see the completion of learning tasks as demonstrating their competence and ability.[10, 13]

When students see learning as incremental and that intelligence is malleable, they are apt to see all challenges as opportunities to learn. They connect learning progress with deliberate practice and effort. They are eager to increase their competence by developing new skills and mastering new situations. They are persistent in the face of failure and use more complex learning strategies. The best learners view successes and failures as internal—*It is up to me!*—and ability as malleable—*I can do something about it!* They believe that ability is not set in stone! And that belief influences their approach to learning.[10,13]

Always strive to build each student's inner voice with signposts. Here's a simple example of a comment on a science paper:

Your diagram included all the important elements of the full water cycle, but you forgot to label each. If you labeled each element, your diagram would be clearer to you and me. I would know for sure that you understood the Water Cycle.

Replace Normative Feedback with Self-Referenced Feedback

Normative feedback is that which compares one learner's performance to that of others. This feedback has a particularly negative effect on learners who perform poorly. They tend to conclude that they just don't have the ability, expect to perform poorly in the future, and are not motivated to attempt subsequent tasks. They just might give up! It has little to no effect on high-performing learners.[10]

You can help low-performing learners respond more constructively to failure or mistakes by expressing feedback in self-referenced terms, that is, relative to their known ability and other factors. With this feedback, learners are not inclined to go into self-protection mode. Rather they hold positive expectations for future performances and connect progress with effort.[10,13]

Here is one more example that distinguishes a constructive way from a defeatist one:

Move from the Situational to the Self-Referential

Rather than expressing feedback normatively: *On this test, the class average was 85%. You scored 50%.*

Express your feedback in self-referenced terms: *On the practice test you scored 25%. On this test, you raised it to 50%, which is a 25% gain! You can raise your performance even more by working on...*

Communicate Effectively with Parents/Guardians

Communication is a message sent and a message received. Not only do parents expect communication with you regarding their children—during conferences with you and via email, for instance—many cite communication as one of the characteristics they most desire in a teacher.

What exactly do parents want you to communicate? Parents want information about how their child is doing in school, and they want that information to be understandable and useful and to include precise information—*data.*

And what *should* you communicate? First and foremost, you must satisfy your parents' need for precise and understandable information. You have an obligation to do so, an obligation that includes documentation—*summative data*—that illustrates a student's performance and progress. You are also in a good position to supply information that you have gained from observing and working with each child. This is *formative data* which you can share about a student's performance and growth.

Supply summative data. First you must gather the data yourself from state test scores, benchmark scores, marking period grades, and even test grades. You must handle the data like this:

- Examine summative data from a variety of available sources.

- Identify data trends as they reveal the student's strengths and areas of weakness.

- Interpret the data and develop hypotheses about how to improve student learning.

- Provide recommendations on how to build on the student's strengths as well as how to improve any weaknesses.

Typically, the best opportunity for sharing summative data is at parent-teacher-student conferences so that you can clarify the meanings of score data and can gauge a parent's comprehension of the implications of the data. Ideally, you and the parent(s) will leave a conference with a plan of action mutually understood and embraced.

Be prepared for difficulties, however, especially if the student is performing poorly in some ways. For instance, parents may be unaware that their child is struggling, or else they may feel ill equipped to handle the problems. They may blame any of a variety of causes for the problems—even you!—so your preparation must include plans of action. This is worth repeating: **Spend ample time prior to a parent conference (or data-sharing event) analyzing summative data, spotting trends, noting strengths and weaknesses, and identifying specific strategies or suggestions for helping that student improve.**

Supply formative data as well. The value of formative data—your observations, your opinions—is its personal nature and the message it conveys that you are actively involved with, concerned, and optimistic about the student. Any communication with parents probably should include your formative data including your current insights as well as your expectations for the student.

This kind of information should focus on the student's current growth as well as prospects for future growth. You may indeed share this kind of information more frequently with parents than simply during parent conferences. You have options for doing this. Here are a few examples:

- Send a celebratory note home after a successful essay.
- Write a quick text to a parent to celebrate the student being on time to class.
- Have on-going email communication regarding a student's growth on reading fluency and comprehension.

This type of communication is a celebration and also a great opportunity to give parents simple strategies that they can use to assist their child.

Current research about effective communication with the home reveals a few more pointers that may be worth keeping in mind during the year:

- Be warm, upbeat, and factual.

- Follow through with promises you make to parents.

- Affirm that parents have valuable knowledge and expertise about their child and that they are equal partners in your work together.

- Honor cultural difference by being aware of how the child's beliefs and values may differ from your own or others in the classroom.

- Practice engaged listening skills.

- Document important parental contacts.

- Convey important information to fellow team members.[1]

RULE OF THUMB: Parents should never be surprised by a grade or summative test score. Keep parents informed via formative data so that your conferences about summative data will be a time to celebrate demonstrable growth (even with a student who has not yet met the expected score).

Consult Experts

1. Black, P. J. and Wiliam, D. "Assessment and Classroom Learning." *Principles, Policy & Practice* 5 (1), 1998.

2. Butler, R. "Task-Involving and Ego-Involving Properties of Evaluation: Effects of Different Feedback Conditions on Motivational Perceptions, Interest, and Performance." *Journal of Educational Psychology* 79 (4), 1987.

3. Hattie, J. and Timperley, H. "The Power of Feedback." *Review of Educational Research* 77 (1), 2007.

4. Hatti, J. *Visible Learning for Teachers: Maximizing Impact on Learning.* New York, NY: Routledge, 2012.

5. Kosmoski, G. J. and Pollack, D. R. *Managing Difficult, Frustrating, and Hostile Conversations: Strategies for Savvy Administrators* (2nd ed.). Thousand Oaks, CA: Sage Publications, 2005.

6. Fisher, D. and Frey, N. "Feed Up, Back, Forward." *Educational Leadership* 67(3), 2009.

7. Moss, C. and Brookhard, S. M. *Learning Targets: Helping Students Aim for Understanding in Today's Lesson.* Alexandria, VA: Association of Supervision and Curriculum and Development, 2012.

8. *My Favorite No: Learning from Mistakes.* Teaching Channel, narrator and teacher, *Leah Alcala*, 29 Nov, 2016.

9. Sadler, R. "Formative Assessment and the Design of Instructional Systems." *Instructional Science* 18: Pages 119 - 144. 1989.

10. Shute, V. J. *Focus on Formative Feedback.* Princeton, NJ: Educational Testing Service, 2007.

11. Smith, I. *Sharing Learning Outcomes.* Cambridge, England: Cambridge Education, 2008.

12. Wiggins, G. "Seven Keys to Effective Feedback." *Educational Leadership* 70 (1), 2012.

13. Wiliam, D. *Embedded Formative Assessment.* Bloomington, IN: Solution Tree Press, 2011.

Self-Assess: Providing Effective Feedback

For each element, self-assess using the following 1-4 scale:

1. **Missing (I need to do this)**
2. **Attempted (I try to do this, but I am not successful)**
3. **Apparent (I do this well, but I don't do it consistently. When I do it, it works!)**
4. **Well Done (I do this consistently and appropriately)**

Focus on Performance Aspects of Product   1 2 3 4
I focus my feedback on precise performance aspects of the
product or task.

Frame Feedback in Context of Learning Outcome   1 2 3 4
I frame my feedback in the context of the learning outcome.

Frame in Context of Sub-skills of Learning Outcome   1 2 3 4
I set realistic times for beginning and ending tasks.

Focus on a Few Important Aspects of Product/Task   1 2 3 4
I focus my feedback to students on critical aspects of the
product or task, but only a few at a time.

Pathway for Forward Action   1 2 3 4
I embed in my feedback a pathway to forward action that
causes students to look at how they might modify their product
or learning to progress toward achieving the full outcome.

Student Reflecting and Thinking on their Products/Tasks   1 2 3 4
I frame my feedback in a way that provokes students to rethink
particular aspects of their product or learning.

Clarification for Students: Where Am I Going? (Feed Up)   1 2 3 4
I visually display and clearly present the learning outcome and
success criteria (sub-skills and concepts) to students at the
beginning of each unit and related lesson.

Clarification: How Am I Going? (Feedback)   1 2 3 4
I provide specific feedback that helps students modify their
learning or product while they can still improve or refine
their work.

Clarification: Where to Next? (Feed Forward)   1 2 3 4
I encourage students to take stock of the work they
have done with an eye toward making it better still.

Clarification: Where to Next? (Feed Forward)   1 2 3 4
I couch my feedback to show students how their
product prepares them for the next challenge coming up.

Feedback at the Process Level   1 2 3 4
I provide feedback that focuses students on processes that
they use to learn new knowledge and skills or to complete
products/tasks.

Feedback at the Self-Regulatory Level   1 2 3 4
I provide opportunities for students to self-assess their own
learning or products they produce and develop forward steps
they can take to improve learning or strengthen/expand products.

Avoiding Feedback at the Self Level   1 2 3 4
I avoid feedback that merely praises the person, e.g. "You're
such a fast learner." Instead, I offer specific examples of what a
student has done well, such as "Your careful study and work
to prepare for this test paid off."

Feedback That Is Self-Referencing   1 2 3 4
I provide feedback that compares students' current performance
with their own past performance rather than with other students'
performances.

Feedback in the Form of Specific Comments   1 2 3 4
I write specific comments on student work in a time frame
that allows for an opportunity to respond prior to final grading.

Time to Respond to Feedback   1 2 3 4
I provide time in class for students to use the specific feedback
to improve their product or process.

To help people meet the new century, planners of the Chicago World's Fair of 1893 introduced millions of visitors to topics that many had barely experienced before. Each topic had its own building like the Electricity Building, the Photography Building, Machinery Hall – each complete with language and special vocabulary that was new to those millions of eyes and ears.

Machinery Hall

Electricity Building

CHAPTER SIX

Treat Content Areas Expansively

Agricultural Building

Manufacturers Building

Know and Convey Content and Language of the Discipline

In a team meeting, Gil Kelton expounded on the issue of teachers NOT mastering their content. "Limited knowledge is a barrier to students' learning!" he declared. "Think like a scholar! Scholars have a thirst for knowledge! Isn't this the habit we strive for students to embrace? Embrace a thirst for knowledge!"

In your classroom everyday, you work hard to ensure students learn. At times their learning is impressive, and other times their struggles leave you frustrated by their lack of progress. Sometimes you may think that students have learned a concept when in actuality you find they have not. Yes, many factors contribute to success, frustration, and failure. You can stay ahead of the game, however, if you keep this idea in mind:

Remind Yourself: My awareness and effectiveness is enhanced or limited by the depth and breadth of my understanding of the content I teach.

"I agree with Gil," Mary Pat said aloud but to no one in particular. "I've been thinking about my own commitment to mathematics. I care deeply. I trained for years always knowing I wanted to teach what I learned."

Dan added, "My content focus begins with key content vocabulary. I make sure I introduce and reinforce terms related to writing: thesis statement, topic sentence, supporting ideas, transition words, coherence …. In math, Mary Pat, your list goes on and on as well."

Your content knowledge affects how you understand concepts, focus content goals, and design lessons that students are expected to master. It affects the way you understand and respond to your students and their questions. It affects your ability to explain clearly and to ask thought provoking questions. It affects your ability to approach a concept in multiple ways and to make connections within and across disciplines. It affects your ability to encourage each student at that optimal moment when he or she is engaged. And it affects your ability to make those moments happen more often for your students.[3]

You can find numerous ways to deepen your content knowledge:

Start or Join a *Content Collaborative*. If you have a content-area team or department that works together regularly, you can use certain tactics to approach this issue with them, or you can start a collaborative group on your own by inviting one or more colleagues to join you in "informal depth sessions" for the purpose of exploring a certain content area for ideas and information to enrich your (and their) lessons.

If you bring specific lessons to your **content collaborative**, or if you focus with them on certain curriculum standards, concepts, and/or skills, you open the door to information sharing—collaborative learning. As you focus on specific concepts related to your curriculum, you can deepen your learning by posing questions:

- *What prior knowledge do students need before this lesson?*
- *What questions will assist student understanding, and what questions will deepen students' thinking?*
- *How does this concept connect with the prior and subsequent concepts?*
- *What other connections will improve understanding?*
- *What are some cross-disciplinary connections that may bring this to life?*
- *Why is this concept important and how does it apply to the real world?*
- *What real life scenarios will help students understand?*
- *Why are we required to teach this concept?"*

Also consider bringing student work to your content collaborative. Analyzing students' work is another way to deepen your content knowledge if your group grapples with the gaps in student mastery and also develops additional content-related ideas for filling those gaps. Surely, discuss the essentials of what students really need to know and push for the nuances—information that can deepen students' understanding (and yours).

Mary Pat's team agreed to increase their efforts to teach their content vocabulary explicitly and to review and assess students' understanding of, and facility with, the language of the discipline.

Be Proactive about Professional Development. Formal professional workshops and courses can improve your knowledge base. But keep in mind that workshops and courses are just the beginning of the learning process. You need to apply and connect newfound knowledge to your curriculum and students. During and after any such event, ask yourself these questions:

- *What are the 3-4 essential ideas that will improve my teaching?*
- *What do I want to focus on first?*
- *How can I apply this content in my classroom?*
- *What goals do I need to set to use this information?*
- *Who will help me apply this new knowledge?*
- *How can I find out more about this content?*
- *What are questions that I still have about this content area?*

Continuing Education. Think of yourself as a scholar who is a professional member of a certain content specialty. Scholars are curious about learning and life. They ask deep questions and seek answers. Scholars ponder ideas and take time to think. They have perseverance, refer to varied resources, set goals, and take risks. You can be a role model for your students, and your very efforts and endeavors at professional growth may affect their learning habits.[3]

Inside the World's Fair Electricity Building, visitors discovered new names like **Westinghouse** and **Tesla** and technical vocabulary like **ampere, wattage, and electrical current**.

Use Language of the Discipline To Engage Students

When an adult says "I'm on a roller coaster" during a hectic period or "You're the light of my life" to show appreciation to his wife, he probably knows he's using a metaphor, and he probably learned the word as well as the concept because the English teacher he no longer remembers used it frequently to bring ideas to life in that class.

To reinforce his points about content vocabulary for his team, Gil added, "A well-known German businessman and entrepreneur, Karl Albrecht, reportedly said this:

'Change your language and you change your thoughts.'"

Part of your knowledge base, including your continuing education, is your familiarity with the specialized terminology of the content area you're teaching, the language of the discipline. Keep that language in mind as you plan lessons so that you incorporate the teaching of academic language (language of the discipline) into your lessons.

Teaching language of the discipline means moving from simplistic words (*body, equal, disappearance*) to sophisticated words (*anatomy, commensurate, extinction*). Your goal is to assist your students in trying to think like a person immersed in the discipline. Ask students to think like a mathematician, like a historian, like a musician, etc. Remember, the skills to encourage are your students' ability to move their language from simple to complex and complex to simple.

Here are a few strategies that you can try in your classroom:

1. Keep a Word Wall or Use a Process for Learning
   Specialized Terms [5]
   a. Have students add a description, explanation,
      or example of each new word.
   b. Have students restate the word in common language.
   c. Ask students to create a picture or symbol
      that represents the term.
   d. Engage students in applying the word in reading
      speaking, writing, performing.

2. Assist Students in Word Study
   Students need to understand syntactic structure,
   vocabulary development, analogies, and etymology
   as well as an appreciation of semantics, linguistics,
   and language history. [7]

3. Provide Students with Academic Text to Translate
   Model how to translate academic text into more
   conventional language. Provide students with an
   academic paragraph that is rich in terminology of

the discipline. Have student teams translate the text using everyday language.

4. <u>Have Students Read Academic Text</u>
   Reading, thinking, and talking about text written in the language of the discipline is an important activity in developing and understanding vocabulary.

"We must make sure that our students use content vocabulary in ways that connect to each of them personally," Gil said.

"I've seen word walls in elementary classrooms, " Mary Pat added, "but it never occurred to me that it would work in middle school."

As their meeting ended, Gil had one last point to make. "We must look for opportunities for each student to use each technical term—visual opportunities like drawings or other representations to clarify the meaning or the work of each term and also aural opportunities like listening to others use key vocabulary terms in vivid ways."

Approach Content in Complex Ways

Simplifying content area terminology may be a noble attempt to make it more accessible for students, but beware of a missed opportunity. You can use specialized terminology as an engagement tactic by asking students to use the language of the discipline in specific ways under your guidance. For instance, have them analyze a topic from global to specific, which will force them to search for word equivalents like synonyms. You can evaluate patterns and trends in passages that use specialized terminology, and you can work with students to examine the unanswered questions raised by the material. Bring into the discussion of new terms some new or different aspects that might be suggested in the passages, such as ethical considerations, generalizations, principles, and theories. Broaden discussion of new terminology by placing it in new contexts in order to examine the past, the present, and ponder the future;

in other words, view the ideas from multiple perspectives, make connections within, among, and across disciplines, and become a content innovator. [1]

Model Critical Thinking for Students

One of the most impactful life gifts that you can offer your students is a challenge to think logically and critically. Students that learn to think critically become self-directed learners who take ownership in their education. Start by modeling critical thinking for your students. Show students how you interact with the content by using thinking processes that analyze content and generate insight into meanings and interpretations. Following is a list of critical thinking skills that might assist you in designing student learning experiences. As you work with students to experience and master new content in a discipline, incorporate challenges for them so that they use new ideas in ways that utilize their thinking variously:

- Inductive reasoning. Move students' thinking from specific observations to broader generalizations and theories.

- Deductive reasoning. Move their thinking from general to more specific confirmation of theory.

- Classifying. Create activities requiring students to sort or group new information according to specific characteristics or qualities that you stipulate for them.

- Sequencing. Have them arrange things or ideas in some kind of series.

- Inferring. Ask students to draw conclusions from facts or premises (again, be sure to include specialized language of the discipline).

- Problem solving. Engage students' thinking skills to solve problems or overcome challenges.

- <u>Patterning.</u> Help them to look for patterns and to use specialized language in their descriptions of those patterns.

- <u>Comparing and contrasting.</u> Create opportunities for students to identify similarities and differences among elements in new information.

- <u>Analyzing.</u> Lead them to find—and to articulate—the relationships among things or ideas, such as part to whole, patterns, sequences, logical deductions, attributes, etc. [2]

Engage Learners in Applying Inquiry and Problem-Solving Skills

Inquiry-based instruction involves engagement, exploration, explanation, extensions, and just plain fun! It differs from typical methods of direct instruction methods because it requires students to discover information, under your guidance of course. Yet it is an ideal method for increasing students' opportunities to treat new content—expansively!

Successful inquiry-based instruction requires you to design and provide the right questions for your students. Here are some questions, by type, that can help you focus the steps in your lessons while expanding students' experiences with the content area:

<u>Engagement Questions</u>
- What do you know about_____?
- What have you seen like this?
- What do you want to know?
- How can you find out?
- What have you learned?

Exploration Questions
- What if . . .?
- How can you best study this question or issue?
- What happens when . . . ?
- What information do you need?
- What method of study should you use?

Explanation Questions
- What pattern(s) did you notice?
- What evidence do you have for your conclusions?
- How can you best explain or demonstrate your findings?
- What are some other explanations for your findings?

Extension Questions
- How do you think____applies to_____?
- What would happen if . . . ?
- Where can we use this concept in the real world?
- What consequences, benefits, and risks will come with this conclusion?
- What unanswered questions do you still have?[4]

"But extension questions are only for language arts and social studies," Mary Pat said to Clay as they discussed her plans for an upcoming lesson that included problem solving.

"These kinds of questions work well in math as well," Clay pointed out, "and science. Can you think of a way to try it?"

Mary Pat decided to construct some "what would happen if ..." questions for her lesson. "I'll have my small groups analyze what would happen to an imaginary student after each step of the problem."

Similarly, you can incorporate several problem-solving models into your plans. If you are new to the problem solving process, look into the researched-based Osborn-Parnes Five Stage Creative Problem Solving Model.[6] It offers an accessible process that you might implement in your classroom. It operates in these stages:

1. Fact-Finding: Discovering and gathering relevant facts.

2. Problem-Finding: Determining the essential problem.

3. Idea-Finding: Generating options and ideas.

4. Solution-Finding: Evaluating ideas with criteria.

5. Acceptance-Finding: Preparing to implement a final solution or idea.

Here's an example of a grade 4 lesson using the Problem Solving Model:

Grade: 4	
Discipline: Social Studies	
Objective 3b: *Analyze how human actions modify the physical environment. Explain viewpoints regarding environmental issues.*	
Fact Finding:	Provide students with resources and means so they can discover and gather relevant facts on how human actions modify the environment. Ask students to view the information from multiple perspectives.
Problem Finding:	Ask students to brainstorm a list of the essential issues related to humans modifying the physical environment and select one essential issue to address.
Idea Finding:	Ask students to brainstorm a list of ideas on how to solve or address the issue of humans modifying the physical environment.
Solution Finding:	Evaluate the ideas or solutions to decide which one would be the best to solve the issue of human modifying the physical environment.
Acceptance Finding:	Prepare a plan to implement the solution or idea.

Use Multiple Representations of Concepts

You can be sure that one or more students will benefit from a visual graphic representation of something. Many are visual learners. Others will gain information efficiently by reading words on a page; others will find auditory explanations useful to them. Another may really "get" an artistic representation of a concept. The point is that variety is your ally in the battle to deliver content mastery. Be sure to provide students opportunities to learn from, examine, and create multiple representations of a concept. In other words, there is not one means of representation that will be optimal for all learners, so providing multiple options will increase comprehension and deepen learning.

And also: Analyze Learner Errors and Misconceptions

Review student work with a discriminating eye, and learn from each student's errors. Determine the reason for the error, and use the data to address the error (or error pattern, if you see one). Be clear about whether a student's error results from a misunderstanding or a miscalculation. You may need to interview the student directly in order to be sure. Error analysis is a "picture" into how well students are understanding content. Use your insight, your error analysis, to guide the student so that you can re-direct, focus, and deepen learning for that student.

Keep Your Content Vocabulary Up Front in Your Planning

As the unofficial scribe for their team, and because Mary Pat is by nature a note-taker, she developed an Action Summary for her team to remind them all—herself included—about the importance of content vocabulary. Here are her six action items:

Six (6) Steps in Planning with Content Vocabulary

1. Research the content related to the curriculum standard to gain greater depth of knowledge to enhance lesson design.

2. Increase the use of key content vocabulary whenever conveying content knowledge to students.

3. Teach key vocabulary explicitly, review it regularly, and assess students' understanding of, and facility with, the terms.

4. Ensure that plans and instructional routines demonstrate accurate and deep understanding of the content and language of the discipline.

5. Align content vocabulary with approved core curriculum standards.

6. Increase opportunities for students to make visual representations of abstract concepts and to interact deeply within text or instruction to connect content vocabulary with him/herself, the world, and prior knowledge. [8]

Consult Experts

1. Kaplan, S. and Gould, B. *Depth & Complexity Icons.* OERI, Javits Curriculum Project, 2003.

2. King, F.J., Goodson, L., and Rohani, F. "Higher Order Thinking Skills: Definition, Teaching Strategies and Assessment." *Assessment & Evaluation: Education Services Program*.http://www.cala.fsu.edu/files/higher_order_thinking_skills. pdf, 1998. online

3. Lappan, G. "Knowing What We Teach and Teaching What We Know." *National Council of Teachers of Mathematics News Bulletin.* http://www.nctm.org/Newand-CalendarMessages-from-the-President Archive/Glenda-Lappan Knowing-What-We-Teach-and-Teaching-What-We-Know/.1999. online

4. Marshall, J. C. "Teaching Through Inquiry: Engage, Explore, Explain, and Extend." *Association for Supervision and Curriculum Development Express* 8 (21), 2013.

5. Marzano, R.J. *Building Background Knowledge for Academic Achievement: Research on What Works in Schools.* Alexandria, VA: ASCD, 2004.

6. Torrance, E.P. and Torrance, J.P. "Developing Creativity: Instructional Materials according to the Osborn-Parnes Creativity Problem Solving Model." *Creative Child and Adult Quarterly*, 1978.

7. VanTassel-Baska, J.L. *Comprehensive Curriculum for Gifted Learners.* Boston, MA: Allyn & Bacon, 1988.

8. *The* TEAM *Research Framework, Teacher Evaluation and Assistance Model.* Bronxville, NY: ObserverTab, LLC., 2016.

Self-Assess: Content Knowledge

For each element, self-assess using the following 1-4 scale:

1. **Missing (I need to do this)**
2. **Attempted (I try to do this, but I am not successful)**
3. **Apparent (I do this well, but I don't do it consistently. When I do it, it works!)**
4. **Well Done (I do this consistently and appropriately)**

Improve my Content Knowledge   1 2 3 4
I continually improve and deepen my content knowledge.

Participate with a Content Study Group   1 2 3 4
I work with a content study group on a regular basis.

Discuss Content in Depth   1 2 3 4
Our study group discusses how to teach each lesson more effectively
by examining essential questions concerning content.

Examine Student Work   1 2 3 4
Our study group examines student work to gain insight on
students' understanding of the content and how to remediate or
extend learning.

Participate in and Apply Content from
Professional Development   1 2 3 4
I participate in content workshops and apply learning into my lessons.

Develop Lessons that Engage Students in the
Language of the Discipline   1 2 3 4
I design lessons that teach students to use the language of
the discipline.

Approach Content in Complex Ways   1 2 3 4
I model and teach critical thinking and engage learners in applying
inquiry and problem solving.

Use Multiple Representation of Concepts   1 2 3 4
I provide opportunities for students to learn and demonstrate learning
through various modes of representation (visual, kinesthetic,
auditory, etc.)

Analyze Learner Errors and Misconceptions   1 2 3 4
I analyze errors and use data to address misunderstandings in order to
redirect, focus, and deepen learning.

New York City's new Second Avenue Subway took not only many years to envision, plan, and complete, but also required the critical thinking of countless engineers, architects, geologists, environmentalists, as well as construction and transportation experts. Its successful outcome stands as proof of the power of ingenuity and the search for new ideas and solutions across the spectrum of human experience.

Engineer Instruction To Go Far and Dig Deep

real-world connections ... higher-order thinking

At a holiday party, Mary Pat sat at a table with Gil, Marge, Dan, and Clay. They had finished eating and were winding down their conversations after sharing good cheer among themselves and with other members of the faculty. They looked on as others left for home and party noises diminished. All five were quiet when Dan spoke to no one in particular, "Do you think we're doing it right?"

Nobody spoke, but Mary Pat and Clay looked at each other. Then he laughed. "Mary Pat probably asks me that question every time I visit her room and every time we debrief!"

"We all wonder if we're getting it right," Marge said.

"Because we care," Clay completed her thought.

"But I'm always wondering if I'm doing enough? Am I doing it well … and thoroughly?" Mary Pat said. "I always plan carefully, but I'm not always sure."

"You're the Master Planner," Clay reminded.

"Seriously, Clay, I don't always know how to plan or where to start or what to look for, especially if it's a new topic …."

"Or even if it's a topic I've taught before," Marge added. "*Especially* if it's a topic I've taught before because I'm afraid of becoming stale or, worse, of leaving out something that's new and important."

The group looked to Gil.

"That's because the world doesn't stand still, Marge," he said. "You know that instinctively. You know that things constantly change, that new things develop all the time, that around every corner is another challenge … or opportunity.

"It's the opportunity that matters," Gil continued. "Like all of us, you know that we can't begin to fathom everything out there, but yet you know it's there, and you desire to use some of it in some new or important way for your students. As long as you feel that way, and as long as you act on it, you are a terrific teacher."

"So how do you define 'opportunity'?" Mary Pat asked Gil. "What do I look for to be on the right track?"

"Opportunity is everywhere," Gil said. "If you know what you want your students to learn, you'll find no shortage of ideas and experiences that you can bring their way, that you can connect them to. Think big, and think 'outside the box' as people younger than I like to say."

"To make new connections for students to the real world," Clay agreed.

"Think outside your own curriculum, even outside your discipline. Help students make connections between curriculum topics and the real-world by leading them to encounter new concepts and skills through their own perspectives and experiences." Gil was warming up.

The group was the last to leave the party.

Plan Lessons To Be Cross-Disciplinary

Mary Pat drove home with this thought: *Life* is interdisciplinary! Learning should be too! She continued to think about what makes a cross-disciplinary learning experience powerful and essential.

Cross-disciplinary lessons engage multiple perspectives and connect students to life experiences, universal themes, issues, questions and topics. Teaching across disciplines involves integrating content, methods, and frameworks from more than one discipline. Students begin to think in broader interconnected perspectives rather than compartmentalized subjects. Instead of teaching only about how patterns assist in solving mathematical problems, for instance, students can begin to understand that the analysis of patterns can assist them in solving all problems—problems in science, for instance, projects in the industrial arts, problems in architecture and engineering.

Discover Real-World Connections across Your Curriculum

Directly related to the challenge, or opportunity, of connecting students to information and experiences outside your discipline, is the limitless supply of those in the world around us. Researchers tell us that finding authentic real-world connections as part of learning experiences can increase student retention of content, develop student interpersonal skills, and improve attitudes toward learning. [3]

Not only can you make such connections for students, but also you can increase the frequency of such connections so that students become accustomed to approaching new things in personal ways. This requires your attention while planning and while on your feet during instruction.

As you address new concepts and skills in your curriculum, plan to connect these to your students' experiences, their prior knowledge, and their intrinsic understandings of things. Finding the best real-world connections requires doing some research, and you will find seemingly unlimited sources:

1. The School Library: For an overview of traditional sources of information, nothing can beat the school library, particularly for students unfamiliar with research. A working knowledge of the dewy decimal system is still a valuable tool! If the librarian is aware of your lesson focus, s/he can take students on a walking tour of the library pointing out the usefulness of diverse informational sources that relate to your topic. Library resources include encyclopedias, dictionaries, thesauruses, biographies, fiction, non-fiction, newspapers, age appropriate magazines, etc. Most libraries also offer access to computers.

2. Media: Local current events and social interactions offer something relevant to any topic imaginable in every content area. The Science section of a major newspaper (don't overlook its archives) can offer a new twist on a required core subject. Editorial cartoons can connect students in personal ways to a topic by inviting them to examine the human side of something. Letters to the editor offer timely thoughts and varying opinions.

3. Local Issues or Events: Your school community offers a wealth of issues that students care about—bullying, new or ineffective rules, sports successes or failures. For instance, you might connect a theme or character in a novel your students are reading to something or someone in your local news. Sometimes, business and government representatives are willing to share information with students through classroom visits or field trips.

Additional resources include parents, neighbors, or other teachers who may have expertise in a real-world problem of interest to your students. Particular students may also have extended information on a topic of interest and may act as leaders to help others learn about the topic at hand. Government and non-profit organizations are often more than willing to send information or even guest speakers to the classroom. Authentic and primary sources provide expert facts and opinions that validate, or refute, a real-world issue.

4. Simulation Sources: Online you will find organizations (commercial, not for profit, and educational) that provide ideas and support for teaching problem-based learning and problem solving. Some require training; some provide information online.

5. The Curriculum: No matter what subject or grade level you teach, your curriculum is filled with real-world problems just waiting for student investigation. Look for unanswered questions and universal issues while reviewing lesson material and while formulating lesson plans. For instance, certain historical figures may have addressed a topic that you plan to introduce. Or a development in art, drama, or music over the years might hold ideas for a student project. A math or science lesson may lead to the design of a school garden. There is just no end to the possibilities.

And here's another possible resource: Barbara Lewis' *Kids' Guide to Social Action*[8] contains useful guidance and offers examples and blank forms that help students write letters, formulate surveys, etc. Some of these ideas may lead you to simple tactics or questions to incorporate into your lessons, while others may inspire projects that include problem-solving strategies which you can address during your work with students.

Plan To Make Real-World Connections to Your Curriculum

Integrating real-world situations into your instruction is a natural way to introduce new concepts and skills because it encourages students to connect what they already know with a new topic. Once your students recognize such connections and apply their background knowledge, it becomes your challenge to take them further through inquiry and exploration into related areas like science, history, math—even works of literature, music, and art!

Recognize the power of your students' interests because you can heighten their engagement by connecting to their lives and experiences. In fact, your ideal goal is to increase the frequency of such connections so that your students become accustomed to approaching new concepts and skills in personal ways. Rely on your resourcefulness and creativity during your lesson planning, and enhance your plans by thinking on your feet during instruction—something that all good teachers do every day.

Help Students Find, Examine, Understand, Analyze, and Evaluate Diverse Sources of Information

Just the amount of information available over the Internet can be overwhelming, so it is critical to guide students as they find, analyze, and use the information available to them. One way to do this is by modeling informational literacy skills. Here are the types of steps that you can take with students:

Steps for Modeling Informational Literacy

1. Identify a real-world situation or problem that students will readily understand, and locate information from a variety of sources.

2. Present students with readings about the situation or problem, and read some of these together to practice examining content.

continued on next page

3. Ask questions to check students' understanding as you examine sources.

4. Have students analyze content by using highlighters, note-taking, or some other device for sorting such things as facts vs. opinion, comparisons and contrasts, orders of importance—whatever discriminators that will help students think critically about these sources.

5. Guide students as they analyze by adding activities that match the task in some way. For instance, you might instruct students to record new vocabulary including "technical vocabulary" related to the real-world situation or problem. Surely ask evaluative questions like "What information do you find helpful? And why?"

6. Guide students in other ways related to critical analysis, such as reminding them that everything presented in a book or on the internet is not always true. Show students how to find information about the authors or sponsors of the information they find. This is very important to accurate, responsible research.

Your modeling not only helps students sharpen their informational literacy, it also helps them to feel comfortable about processing resources on their own.

Infuse Your Daily Lessons with Real-World Connections

Some of your real-world connections can be quick and easy. Almost every teacher makes an assortment of such connections every day. Teaching patterns in mathematics, for instance, a kindergarten teacher might meet that standard by creating a task that students can relate to from prior experience. Or a sixth grade teacher might connect new vocabulary to a writing activity. Or a high school teacher might introduce a history unit about an ancient society by making connections to similarities in current-day society. Here's how these teachers did it:

Real-World Connection (Kindergarten)

Teacher shows an unfinished bracelet to the class. "Now watch what I do. First I put on a red bead. Then I put on a green bead and then a blue bead. When I put on a red bead, I am starting the pattern again: red, green, blue. If this pattern continues, what color will my eleventh bead be?" Make your own bead bracelet by making a new pattern. Then share your pattern with a partner.

Real-World Connection (Sixth Grade)

To prepare for a vocabulary test, a sixth grade teacher displays four of the hardest words and asks students to write a persuasive paragraph about a current topic. For instance, to connect vocabulary to a novel students are reading, she asks students to write about one of the characters in the novel using any four of these five words in any of their forms: *expanse, prominent, tortuous, inundate, jaunt.*

Real-World Connection (Ninth Grade)

To introduce ancient Egypt, a history teacher displays pictures of artifacts (e.g., tools, utensils, urns, ruins, hieroglyphs) and asks each student to sketch two or three of the objects and to write an assumption about the purpose or use of each, identifying modern day objects that are possibly similar in purpose. For instance, a long piece of flint might have been useful then as today's fork, or a woven basket with a long pole through it might today be useful as a wheel barrel or a shopping cart. To check their assumptions, each student must search resources about ancient Egyptian artifacts.

No end exists to the possibilities you can find for infusing lessons with relevant real-world situations.

Develop Sequenced Lesson and Unit Plans with Real-World Connections

Developing a sequence of lessons or an entire unit requires more deliberate—and more extensive—planning.

Often, your plan begins with a Learning Outcome followed by sections devoted to Materials, Preparation, Motivation, Discussion, Introduction, Steps, Applications, Assessment, Reflections, and so forth. But how do you plan to make real-world connections as you formulate each part of your plan?

Following is an example of one teacher's plan to incorporate real-world connections into a social studies lesson (the right column). The left column identifies the kinds of questions this teacher asked herself as she planned the lesson.

Lesson Planning for Real-World Connections

Questions To Ask Myself	My Lesson Plan (Partial)
	Curriculum: American Studies
	Subject: *The Bill of Rights*
Which of the freedoms will feel relevant to my students?	**Lesson Topic:** Freedoms in *The Bill of Rights*
	Learning Outcome: Students will understand the First Amendment guarantee of freedom of speech, learn about a landmark case supporting the freedom of speech, and engage in a debate about the extent to which freedom of speech rights should apply to students. They will demonstrate their understanding in an essay at the end of the unit.

continued on next page

What kinds of stories, quotes, or situations will catch the interests of my students?	**Motivation:** Quote: *"I disapprove of what you say, but I will defend to the death your right to say it."* Situation: *In 1965, John Tinker, his sister Mary Beth, and a friend were sent home from school for wearing black armbands to protest the Vietnam War. The school had a policy permitting students to wear political symbols but had excluded the wearing of armbands protesting the war. Their father sued the school board.*
What key, open-ended questions will invite students to think and respond?	**Discussion:** Begin with these questions: *What is freedom of speech?* *Does freedom of speech improve society?* *How?* *Should there be limits to what we can say?* *Should teenagers have the same rights as adults?* *Have you ever felt silenced from speaking? How?*
What diverse sources of information should students find, examine, understand, analyze?	**Research:** Provide a copy of the First Amendment. Have students examine, understand, and analyze the Amendment. Ask students to use words in the amendment to explain their answers to discussion questions. (Note: Do not yet tell students the verdict in the *Tinker v. Des Moines* case.)
What activities will engage students in a real-world problem or situation?	**Problem Solving:** Have students re-enact arguments from *Tinker v. Des Moines* by dividing students into three groups: (1) Tinker, (2) Des Moines, and (3) Supreme Court justices. Have groups 1 and 2 present their cases; group 3 makes a judgment on the cases that group 1/group 2 presented.

continued on next page

What questions will help students engage in a real-world problem or situation?	**Reflection:** Provide copies of the First Amendment and read the real verdict. Ask students the following reflection questions: *Do you agree with the verdict? Why? Why not?* *How does the decision affect you today?* *How has the case changed your thinking?*
What questions will help students think about the importance of a real-world problem or situation related to their own lives?	**Application:** Have students brainstorm issues that they are passionate about today. Ask them to develop a way to express opinions about an issue at school using the Supreme Court interpretation of the First Amendment.
How can I assess students' understanding?	**Assessment:** Students will complete an essay: *What is Freedom of Speech; when and why is it protected? Discuss positive and negative aspects of the freedom. Tell how it impacts your life today.*

Plan Extended Projects That Access Real-World Knowledge

You can go even further by having students tackle longer-term projects that challenge them to gather and build, sort and create, evaluate and finalize. And when all of the pieces they work with interact across a variety of content areas, the result is true, effective cross-curricular teaching and learning.

While your project must accommodate the essential elements of a good plan (e.g., a focused subject and specific learning outcomes, motivation, research opportunities), you must also provide opportunities for students to solve problems in active ways—to try tactics they may never have tried before, such as making phone calls, writing letters, creating surveys or proposals, soliciting information or involvement from community members.

Here is another example of planning with real-world situations and problems in mind, this one for an extended project:

Project Planning for Real-World Connections

Questions To Ask Myself	My Lesson Plan (Partial)
	Curriculum: Utah Studies
	Subject: Migration
	Lesson Topic: Communication needs of immigrant students new to Utah
What did immigrants to Utah need or want that immigrants to the U.S. today also need or want?	**Learning Outcomes:** During Utah studies, students will understand how immigrants from early Utah pioneers to immigrant students today need support while learning to communicate in a new environment. In addition, they will recognize the exciting contributions immigrants bring to a society.
How can I make this topic relevant to my students?	**Motivation:** Quote: **Referring to the newly created Deseret Alphabet being used in schools, Brigham Young said this:** "It [the Deseret Alphabet] will be the means of introducing uniformity in our orthography, and the years that are now required to learn to read and spell can be devoted to other studies."
What stories, quotes, or situations will catch the interests of my students?	**Situation:** *Early immigrants to Utah included people from many countries. They brought skills and abilities that greatly benefited early communities in important ways. But as a number of immigrants did not speak English, Brigham Young recognized the difficulties faced with so many people trying to learn a new language, so he ordered the creation of a new alphabet where each sound had its own symbol, which helped the immigrants to learn to read and write English in a way that could be more phonetically consistent and easier for immigrants to learn. An example of the creation of another common language is American Sign Language.*

continued on next page

What key, open-ended questions will invite students to think and respond?

Research: Provide a copy of the Deseret Alphabet to students. (You may call it a secret code, but don't give any background information.) Ask students to study the document to figure out what it is and how it might be used. Then ask students to write a word or short sentence using the symbols and to compare and contrast this document with the English alphabet. Encourage students to consider vowel sounds, and how this language tried to make English easier to understand.

Review or study the mass migration to Utah in the mid 1800s. Discuss how important these immigrants were to the population with their varied skills and talents. Recognize that as well as bringing new life and ideas to the community, it was difficult for non-English speaking people to understand their new environment. Imagine what it might be like to be in a class where students did not speak the same language. How would you feel? How might this affect your ability to fit into the routine of the class and make friends? Would you work harder, or just give up?

What activities will engage students in a real-world problem or situation?

Problem Solving: Discuss how Brigham Young attempted to help immigrants new to Utah feel more comfortable and adjust to the culture by creating the Deseret Alphabet. Compare and contrast communication needs in 1840s with the needs of immigrant students today. Instruct students to compose appropriate interview questions that will help them better understand the difficulties faced by students learning a new language. Ask students to write a letter requesting willing students, parents, or the English

continued on next page

as a Second Language teacher to visit the classroom, explain their experience, answer student questions, and brainstorm with them as they consider ways to help immigrant students new to the school. Complete several interviews to gain a better idea of how students in the school might support new non-English speaking students, as well as how these students can be allowed to share their unique culture and heritage to enrich the classroom.

What questions will engage students in a real-world problem or situation?

Reflection: *How does the situation facing Utah immigrant school children in the 1840's compare with the difficulties faced by student immigrants today?*

Why do you think the Deseret Alphabet didn't work? What might have worked better?

After this study, do you feel differently about the importance of communication in your life and in the lives of those around you? How has this experience changed your thinking?

What questions will help students think about the importance of a real-world problem or situation related to their own lives?

Application: Using what they have learned, ask students to take the lead in this real-world problem by brainstorming ways they can help non-English speaking students adjust, have friends, and receive support while they are learning English. (You may wish to share student ideas with the principal, other teachers, and the PTA in hopes of encouraging support throughout the school.)

How can I assess students' understanding?

Assessment: Each student will write a letter to an official or school administrator offering opinions regarding the importance of supporting and celebrating immigrants from the past to the present concluding with a solution to how their school can support and celebrate new non-English speaking students today.

Guide Your Students as They Work with Real-World Contexts

The success of your plans depends in part on the types and frequency of your facilitation. That is, the more actively you interact with all phases of student work, the more successful your students will be. This is especially true with lessons relying on real-world contexts that broaden students' understanding.

Here are some guidelines for helping student maximize real-world contexts:

1. Be a facilitator more than an instructor. Your job is to help students plumb their own understanding and experiences in order to gain new knowledge.

2. Stand ready to be each student's research assistant so that you can suggest pathways and resources.

3. Elicit student discourse as they work. Ask them questions. Have them ask questions of each other.

4. Use open-ended questions only when it's advisable to spark interest and to motivate discussion.

5. Prepare teacher-guided, interactive activities that engage students collaboratively in completing a task. Your strategy is to design a series of questions and activities that lead students to take more and more responsibility to think and solve.

6. Be prepared to hold ad hoc brainstorming sessions to help students stay on track, overcome confusion, or correct course.

Recognize Opportunities To Enhance Cognition

Primers of old exhorted students to learn facts—their A,B,Cs, dates, names—and their teachers focused on rote memory techniques to learn those facts. Over decades, the experiences and explorations of legions of educators led to insights and techniques that we have on hand today. An important part of our work now is to teach students how to think critically and deeply (and of course, facts still matter).

Research and practice offer opportunities to grow your repertoire of techniques. For instance, we know that questioning and tasking of students can be scaffolded according to types of questions we pose and by the levels of knowledge embedded in the wording of those requests. Also, we know that real-world contexts offer myriad opportunities for evaluating, analyzing, and synthesizing information in order to make decisions and to create original work.

Access Higher Order Thinking

Let your questions and tasks add rigor by engaging deeper levels of thought. As you plan tasks for your student via your questions and your engagement requests, think about the specific mental actions that your students need to take in order to answer properly. Yes, many of your questions will begin with *Who, What, When, Where,* and these commonly lead toward simple recall, which is a fairly easy mental activity. Either the student knows the answer or he doesn't. And the word *Why* may dig a bit deeper if it requires some Level 2 or 3 mental activity.

But you can dig deeper. A careful choice of verb—in combination with words that complement that verb—can be your secret weapon. Embedded in certain verbs are mental requirements that offer clues to students about how to engage their brains. Here are examples:

- The verb *compare* alerts the student that he has to consider two disparate things.
- *Summarize* requires him to consider even more variables.
- A verb like *estimate* tells your thinker that the answer probably won't be a simple, finite, one-size-fits-all concept but rather one that he has to handle qualitatively.

The right verb can be your good friend if you associate it with the right words that complete the action of the verb and lead your students toward the outcome you expect. Here is a list of really good verbs to plant within your engagement requests:

Verbs That Engage
Level One (Recall): Arrange, Calculate, Define, Draw, Identify, List, Label, Illustrate, Measure, Memorize, Repeat, Recall, Recite, State, Tell, Tabulate, Recognize, Name, Use, Report, Quote, Match.
Level Two (Skill/Concept Comprehension): Infer, Categorize, Collect and Display, Identify Patterns, Organize, Construct, Modify, Predict, Interpret, Distinguish, Use Context Clues, Make Observations, Summarize, Show, Graph, Classify, Separate, Cause/Effect, Estimate, Compare, Relate.
Level Three (Analytic Thinking): Revise, Assess, Connect, Develop, Apprise, Construct, Compare, Formulate, Investigate, Draw Conclusions, Differentiate, Hypothesize, Cite Evidence.
Level Four (Synthesis): Design, Synthesize, Apply Concepts, Critique, Analyze, Create, Prove.
Information in this chart may help frame questions and tasks as analyzed and defined by researchers such as Karin Hess, Norman Webb, and others.

Re-word for Rigor

Your words also can deepen the rigor of your request. By phrasing some requests with words of action tied to deeper levels of thought (e.g., a statement conveyed with level-three or –four verbiage), and by selecting an appropriate strategy or structure for student participation, such as a type of student-to-student task, you can create a framework for each student to access deeper levels of thinking to handle the task. Here are some examples of re-wording. See if you think the Higher-Level Requests add rigor to each task and increase student interest:

Re-Wording Your Requests To Enhance Rigor		
Lower Level Request	Rewording Strategy	Higher Level Request
Name the world's 7 continents.	**Change a recall task to an analytic task.** Add a thinking verb (predict). Specify task structure (group work).	*In your group, predict how continental drift will change the future locations of the continents.*
Summarize General Grant's strategy in the battle of Gettysburg.	**Change a skill/ concept task to a synthesis task.** Add or modify a factor. Specify task structure.	*Hypothesize how one change in the Confederate strategy could have altered the outcome. Defend your hypothesis to your partner.*
Identify a number under 100 that has many factors.	**Change a skill/ concept task to a synthesis task.** Enlarge task to include a higher-level skill. Specify task structure.	*With a team, find the numbers under 100 that have many factors. Design a question about these number patterns that will deepen our understanding of factors.*
Infer how the main character feels about 2 other characters in the story.	**Change a skill/ concept comprehension task to one that combines analysis and synthesis.** Add another dimension to the problem.	*With a partner, create a diagram to compare and contrast how the main character and two other characters feel about each other. Add evidence into your diagram.*

Consult Experts

1. Ambrose, S. A., Bridges, M. W., DePietro, M., Lovett, M. C., and Norman, M. K. *How Learning Works: Seven Research-based Principles for Smart Teaching.* San Francisco, CA: Jossey-Bass, 2010.

2. Costa, A.L. and Garmston, R.J. *Cognitive Coaching: A Foundation for Renaissance Schools.* Foxboro, MA: Christopher-Gordon Publishers, 1994.

3. Davenport, M. "Asking Essential Questions To Inspire Lifelong Learning." Rubicon Educational Foundation, 2017. online

4. Drake, S.M. *Curriculum Handbook: Integrated Curriculum.* Alexandria, VA: ASCD, 2000.

5. Fisher, D. and Frey, N. "Show & Tell: A Video Column/Transfer Goals for Deeper Learning." *Educational Leadership* 73 (6), 2016.

6. Forlini, G., Williams, E., and Brinkman, A. *Class Acts: Your Guide To Activate Learning.* Bronxville, New York: Lavender Hill Press, 2016.

7. Gardner, H. *Multiple Intelligences.* New York: Harper- Collins, 1993.

8. Lewis, B. *The Kid's Guide to Social Action: How to Solve the Social Problems You Choose and Turn Creative Thinking into Positive Action.* Minneapolis, MN: Free Spirit Publishing, 1998.

9. McTighe, J. and Wiggins, G. *Essential Questions: Opening Doors to Student Understanding.* Alexandria, VA: ASCD, 2013.

10. McTighe, J. and Wiggins, G. *Improve Curriculum, Assessment, and Instruction Using the "Understanding by Design" Framework.* Alexandria, VA: ASCD, 2014.

11. McTighe, J. and Wiggins, G. *Understanding by Design.* Alexandria, VA: ASCD, 2005.

12. Polya, G. *How To Solve It*, 2nd ed. Princeton, NJ: Princeton University Press, 1957.

13. Smith, M. K., et. al. "Why Peer Discussion Improves Student Performance on In-Class Concept Questions." *Science* 323. 5910: Pages 122-124.017.

Self-Assess: Achieving Depth through Real-World Connections and Enhanced Cognition

For each element, self-assess using the following 1-4 scale:

1. **Missing** (I need to do this)
2. **Attempted** (I try to do this, but I am not successful)
3. **Apparent** (I do this well, but I don't do it consistently. When I do it, it works!)
4. **Well Done** (I do this consistently and appropriately)

Planning for Cross-Disciplinary Opportunities 1 2 3 4
I explore related disciplines (math, science, social studies, the arts, etc.) for information and experiences that will enhance my instruction and will enable students to broaden their understanding.

Planning for Real-World Applications 1 2 3 4
My planning includes locating, identifying, and incorporating real-world problems, situations, and tasks into my instruction.

Applying Real-World Situations to New Concepts and Skills 1 2 3 4
I connect real-world problems and situations to the specific concepts and skills in my curriculum standards.

Teaching Problem-Solving Strategies 1 2 3 4
I teach real-world problem solving strategies by giving examples and facilitating student practice.

Building Students' Problem-Solving Skills 1 2 3 4
I help students select real-world problems and situations for their projects using such things as local issues or events, media, simulation, or problems derived from the curriculum.

Providing Resources for Students 1 2 3 4
To expand students' informational literacy, I find and provide a variety of resources to aid students in examining, understanding, analyzing, and evaluating real-world problems and situations.

Guiding Students' Independent Work and Projects　　1 2 3 4
I plan and use open-ended questioning and guided tasks to
facilitate students' success incorporating real-world problems
and situations into their work products.

Assessing Student Learning　　1 2 3 4
As students interact with real-world problems and situations
connected to our standards, I use their authentic products as
well as traditional forms of assessment to determine student
learning and growth.

Enhancing Cognition　　1 2 3 4
I plan tasks and questions for students that will lead them to
higher-order thinking and application of the information and
experiences in focus through various modes of representation
(visual, kinesthetic, auditory, etc.)

1903 Wright Bros. Plane Source: Bignoti.com

Early aviation designers like the Wright brothers scrutinized the movements of birds in flight to gain insight into their unique abilities. From those observations, they drew initial plans for flying machines and redesigned those plans. Indeed, the term "aviation" itself begins with the Latin prefix "avis," which means "bird," and ends with "ation," which means "the result of an instance of an action."

Design Responses to Individual Needs

*learning styles ... feedback ... choice
perseverance ... metacognition*

Discover Learner Differences

Viola engaged a speaker for a professional development day, a research/practitioner she had met at an ASCD conference. The speaker began by displaying this question for all to ponder:

Does every child have a unique learning mechanism?

After he listened to opinions from the audience, he began, "Traditionally, our educational system has organized pre-K12 students based primarily on age, encouraging teachers, administrators, and parents to make the false assumption that if students are basically the same age, then they are at the same readiness level to learn.

"Nothing could be further from the truth," he continued, "because students come to school with widely varying levels of readiness, interests, learning profiles, prior formal and informal learning experiences—all of which dramatically influence their learning going forward.

"For these reasons, teachers today recognize the need to **differentiate instruction** so that they can help each student learn maximally, but they recognize also that differentiating effectively is not a simple task.

"For you, and for every other teacher, effective differentiation begins with discovering each student's *'learning mechanism,'* which requires using continuous formal and informal assessment practices to identify, or discover, each student's readiness levels, interests, and learning profile. Your discovery work rests on two initial protocols:

"1. Fashion your learning environment in ways that keep expected procedures and outcomes in sharp relief while (a) fostering respect and rapport among all, and (b) holding high expectations for each student, and

2. Design lessons that embed diverse tasks and products while offering choices, or a variety of pathways, for students to achieve mastery."

Note: Fully differentiated instruction encompasses still more strategies that you can find for creating varied learning experiences (Chapters 1 and 2), using data and feedback to differentiate instruction (Chapter 5), managing self-directed learners, and, maximizing student engagement (see *Class Acts: Your Guide To Activate Learning*).

Fashion Your Environment To Support Diverse Styles

Education researchers such as Tomlinson believe that the classroom environment engenders in each student a positive or negative affect. If the affect is negative, one student may feel unsafe to take the risk of learning new things; another student may feel alienated, while yet another student may feel disrespected. If the affect is positive, students more readily engage in the risk of learning hard things, feel included in the community of learners, and hold an expectation that they will succeed. Tomlinson posits that "affect" is the gateway to students' willingness to fully engage and succeed in learning.[20]

Your understanding of current research will help you shape your planning, your physical and emotional classroom environment, and your daily protocols. These are the preliminary, most basic steps that researchers suggest:

1. Establish expectations for three or four critical long-term behavioral habits that support learning in most situations.

2. Include students in shaping life in your classroom by involving them in the focus and management of key protocols.

3. Develop specific feedback for your students to help each understand his or her direction and progress.

Hold High Expectations of Students

Always begin to establish expectations on day one because your expectations can effectively communicate highly significant things to your students: (1) that you care intently about how they perform, (2) that you believe that each student can meet your expectations, and (3) that the behaviors within your expectations will lead to successful learning. It doesn't hurt to point out these very ideas, by the way.

Plan to begin the year by introducing those three or four critical long-term behaviors that you believe will have the highest impact on student success. Ask yourself this:

Considering the learning experiences I wish to provide my students, what three to four behavioral habits must they develop to succeed?

For instance, you might teach habits to your students for using equipment or learning centers, or you might teach protocols for working in partners or small groups while you conduct conferences or provide small group instruction.

For your students to prosper, they will need to internalize a few critical habits that are unique to your classroom and/or your content area. Below are a few critical habits that one teacher established for her students:

Critical Behavior #1: Your Daily Bell-Ringer Leads to Increased Understanding

Habit 1: Self-start on the Bell Ringer immediately after you enter the room.

Habit 2: When you have completed one task, begin working on another immediately without being told.

Habit 3: Move silently with intent.

Habit 4: Raise your hand and wait to be called on during the discussion that follows.

Teach each of your expectations by following a clear process which normally takes 15-20 minutes. Be sure to follow through on each process during subsequent days. Teach a second expectation on a different day. Teaching one habit per day and following through with it is more effective than addressing all four habits at once. Here is one procedure that has worked:

First, communicate that something important is about to happen. Change the setting. Move students to another setting or completely clear off desks. Take an expert stance by communicating a businesslike demeanor and voice. Treat the teaching of this habit as serious business, not a game.

Use a four-step process to teach the habit. The book *Class Acts* describes in detail how teachers set expectations through a stepwise approach and follow-through with support over time.[4] In brief, a four-step process proceeds this way:

Four-Step Process To Teach a Habit

Step One: <u>Describe the habit</u>. Introduce the habit and tell students why it is important. In a brief activity that you facilitate with students, develop a chart that shows what your expectation, or their eventual habit, will "Look Like" and "Sound Like."

Step Two: <u>Demonstrate</u>. Select a few students to demonstrate the habit the wrong way and the right way.

Step Three: <u>Practice with everybody</u>. Set up a situation that calls for the habit and have everybody practice it the right way.

Step Four: <u>Maintain</u>. Use support skills like proximity and positive cueing to maintain the habit.

Instill the Habit from Day One. Noted philosopher William James commented on establishing a habit, "Never suffer an exception to occur until the new habit is securely rooted in your life." This should apply to your process as well. Once your students have learned the habit, use it every time it is required. For instance, if you are an elementary teacher who expects students will self-start at the beginning of the day, after each recess and after lunch, be sure you provide a self-start for them at each of those times. If you are a secondary teacher who tells students they will have a self-starter (bell ringer) at the beginning of each class, be sure you provide one. Otherwise, you will teach your students that these habits are not important and they will soon slack off.

Maintain the Habit over Time. Proximity and positive cueing are two practices that help students maintain critical behavioral habits. Using **proximity**, you visually scan the room regularly whether addressing the whole class or working with small groups of students. You locate and relocate yourself strategically, which discourages disruptions before they gain momentum, and you establish a felt presence (visually and physically) that, by itself, discourages off-task behavior and encourages engagement.

Using **positive cueing**, you offer specific feedback statements that give information to students of what exactly they are doing correctly. For example, a positive cue for self-starting on a bell ringer activity could be this: *By the time the second bell rang, 27 out of 28 of you had your pencils and paper out and had written down the first problem.* When you are adept at using visual and physical proximity, you are positioned to notice the good things that students are doing and can give descriptive positive cues to students at the individual, small group, or whole group level. Public positive cues that are authentic have a ripple effect in that they motivate more students to exhibit the focus behavior, particularly in younger grades or in the classrooms of well-regarded teachers. The more descriptive and specific the positive cue (feedback) is, the more it promotes students meeting that expectation.

Students need a safe purposeful setting to succeed. Kounin observed that teachers whose lack of effective proximity regularly allows misbehavior to ripple throughout the class before intervening, tend to use intemperate means like scolding to get students to settle down and work.[11] But since good behavior under duress doesn't last long, these teachers continue to yell or threaten punishment to bring students back to order causing some students consciously or unconsciously to withdraw from learning.

On the other hand, students whose teachers teach and hold students to high behavioral expectations through supportive means are more successful in creating positive, safe environments for learning. Students' optimism toward learning grows with a teacher who creates an inclusive culture for learning.

Create an Inclusive Culture for Learning

Culture consists of beliefs, values, and assumptions, all which shape the way it manifests visually in *"the way we do things here."* Teachers communicate their learning culture in words, actions, body language, voice tone, and myriad other subtle ways. They shape instruction and interact with students based on their values, assumptions, and beliefs about children as learners. If the culture is inclusive and supportive, students feel a significant part of the community of learners. They approach learning with the expectation of success.

Knowing that much of culture is communicated through unconscious powerful nuances, you can shape your classroom culture with intentionality in large and small ways. For instance, you can systematically include students in making authentic decisions that relate to how students will behave and interact with each other. You can consciously tailor feedback that enhances students' behavioral and academic performance, including opportunities for students to self-assess their own endeavors. Here are a few processes you can use to create inclusiveness:

Co-Develop Classroom Norms with Your Students. Unlike typical classroom rules, which are developed to establish order or long-term habits that support learning, norms are standards of interaction among people in an environment. Generally speaking, norms exist whether a teacher directly addresses them or not. For example, most people take turns, even though it is not posted as a rule.

John McCartney suggests that including students in directly identifying and committing to norms for how to function with each other in their learning community will lead to enhanced student learning and development.[13] Here is a procedure similar to the one he suggests:

1. Give students think time to reflect on other positive communities they've been members of that affected them

positively (past classrooms, sports groups, family, group of friends, scout groups, etc.)

2. Have students work in groups to *identify* behaviors that made these communities so positive. List them on a large chart.

3. Use *Think-Pair-Share* to generate positive behaviors that would support a learning environment where everybody feels included, supported and successful; students will write each behavior down on sticky notes—one behavior per sticky note.

4. In small groups of 3-5, have students pool their sticky notes and categorize them into like behaviors. Select the 3-5 categories with the largest number of sticky notes to take to the next step.

5. Have each group generate a norm statement for each of their 3-5 largest categories, such as *Everybody's ideas matter! We don't do put-downs here!* Chart their norm statements on a large chart paper and post on walls where all students can see.

6. Involve students in team-building. After each task, ask students to think of the behavioral skills they needed to complete the task successfully.

7. After students have engaged in several team-building activities, have them identify 4-5 norms they would commit to following so each student feels valued and successful. Record each norm on a large poster in positive student-friendly language and post in a visible place where all students can see.

8. Support students to internalize these norms into their behavior over time through specific positive feedback and individual and group self-reflection.

9. Celebrate success!

Build Your Culture through a "Behavioral Garage Sale." School culture experts Deal and Peterson recommend holding a cultural garage sale to eliminate negative cultural elements and to keep positive cultural elements—essentially sorting behaviors for retention and elimination.[2] A process like this may require two to three sessions to complete and can be adapted to help students sort through their behaviors to identify the keeper behaviors and to eliminate the loser behaviors. This works well with elementary-age students and can be focused for secondary. Here is one process you might conduct with students:

1. **Introduce the Goal.** Ask students to think about all different ways we behave with each other during and outside of class time. Point out that positive behaviors such as including each other in games, contribute to making each of us feel included, supported, and successful while negative behaviors impact our feelings of personal value. Then introduce the idea of planning a "garage sale" to keep positive behaviors and eliminate negative ones.

2. **Take Inventory of Existing Behaviors.** Organize students in groups of 3-4 and provide each with 5-10 large paper strips and a magic marker to list positive and negatives ways they behave toward each other, one behavior per strip. Put behavior strips up on the board for all to see.

3. **Establish Criteria for Sorting Behaviors.** To help students quickly identify "keepers" and "losers," give them a set of simple criteria like this:

Criteria for "Keeping" Behavior

This behavior …
- supports students to succeed.
- helps students feel included.
- makes students feel accepted.

---

4. **Identify Keepers and Losers**. As you read each behavior, have students respond in one of these three ways and place the paper strip under corresponding categories. "Sorting bins" might be labeled *Thumbs Up*, *Thumbs Down*, *Not Sure* or any other sorting language. As students respond to each behavior, move it into its proper sorting bin.

5. **Articulate Cultural Norms.** Once students have several behaviors in the *Thumbs Up* bin, ask them to form a statement for each of them (you might combine similar behaviors) that presents the behavior(s) as a valuable, positive interaction.

Naturally, your goal is to internalize these norms into your students' behaviors over time through specific positive feedback as well as individual and group self-reflection. To this end, you might keep your cultural norms posted in a visible location within the classroom. Engaging students in these and similar decision-making processes communicates your respect and positive regard for students' ideas while giving them voice. Conditions like these open students up, physically and emotionally, to engage in learning difficult things with the hope of succeeding.

Provide Effective Feedback

Hattie and Timperley found that of 138 practices that impacted learning, effective feedback was in the top 5 to 10 of greatest impact. Well-crafted feedback enhances the positive culture of your classroom by giving students actionable information on nearly every aspect of classroom life.

Feedback can be given by the teacher, co-generated by students, and produced through individual student self-assessment. Feedback can greatly enhance the culture of your classroom and students' academic learning, but it must be delivered effectively.

In his work on embedded formative assessment, Wiliam gives us three principles for effective feedback that enhances student learning and development:[22]

1. **Frame your feedback relative to the desired outcome**. Develop, post, and present a learning target with success criteria that communicate the sub-units of behavior or knowledge that lead to success. Present this information to students at the outset and keep it posted during the acquisition of the behaviors, norms, or academic endeavors. Then as you give feedback to individuals, direct them to the specific aspects they've mastered and point to modifications they can make strategically to achieve the targeted outcome.

2. **Give focused feedback**. As you look at students' performance, focus your feedback only on a few key aspects of an attempt in order to give them just enough information that they can see where to improve and how to go about it with confidence.

3. **Use feedback to provoke forward action**. If your feedback causes your learner to think about ways to modify his or her actions, then you're on your way to success. Good feedback contains a pathway to forward action for students to help them progress toward the desired outcome.

Apply feedback directly into your work of creating a high-functioning learning culture. For instance, if you are teaching a long-term habit like self-starting, you and your students might co-develop a chart like the following to detail what effective self-starting looks like and sounds like:

Behavior Outcome: *I can start myself on work immediately when I enter the classroom.*

Success Criteria: *I will know I can self-start perfectly when I see myself ...*
- enter room quietly, put coat and supplies away.
- go right to desk.
- read through self-starter.
- start and sustain work on self-starter immediately.
- link to another piece of work once the self-starter is completed.

Perfect Self-Starting Sounds Like ...
- quiet working.
- sound of pencils or pages turning.

And consider these additional examples of feedback as suggested by Wiliam's work:

Frame your feedback relative to the desired outcome:
Students, I can see that you are working to develop the habit of self-starting by how quietly you entered the room, read through, and immediately started work on your self-starter. Know that this habit will enhance your learning this year as well as in future schooling, getting and keeping a job, and accomplishing personal goals. This is an important life habit.

Give Focused Feedback. *Students, as I observe you self-start, I can see that you have pretty much mastered these parts: enter the room quietly, read through the self-starter, and immediately begin and sustain your work on the self-starter. As a group, you are approaching mastery on transitioning to the next topic once you've completed the self-starter. Some of you make that transition perfectly, but quite a few of you engage in side conversations.*

Use feedback to provoke forward action: *You've internalized all aspects of self-starting beautifully. One area that we could clean up is "linking to the next task" once we've completed the self-starter. Some ideas you might consider are these: 1. make a list of assignments you could work on, 2. put materials for the next task on your desk ahead of time, 3. think in your mind, "What are some strategies I could use?" (Pause while students think.) Share them with your across-the-table partner.*

Feedback that follows Wiliam's principles clarifies and motivates students to meet critical behavioral expectations. It communicates to them that behavior is developmental and that they can do things to strengthen that behavior. To make this feedback even more effective, use a professional but approachable voice, and communicate receptivity through your body language.[22]

Here is an example of providing feedback at the self-regulatory level by engaging your students in the meta-cognitive process of self-assessing their behavioral, normative, and academic efforts. These norms become the Desired Outcome and Success Criteria that you would post prominently in your room:

Classroom Norms

Desired Outcome: *We commit to interacting with each other in ways that help each of us to feel valued, supported, and successful.*
Success Criteria: *We know we are successful when we …*
- value each other's ideas.
- listen to what each other says.
- avoid put-downs.
- include each other in games and working groups.
- show respect for each other's cultures and backgrounds.

And here is one way you might set students up to self-reflect on the degree to which they are following the norms they have co-established. Hand each a piece of paper with the following self-reflection:

Classroom Norms

Desired Outcome: I am learning to interact with my classmates in ways that make them feel *valued, supported, and successful.*

I will evaluate my progress by circling the number that indicates the degree to which I do the following:

1 = I am beginning to develop that behavior.

2 = I usually exhibit that behavior.

3 = I consistently exhibit that behavior, and I am working to refine it.

4 = I exhibit that behavior perfectly with rare exception.

Success criteria-specific norms to which I have committed:

• Value each other's ideas.	1	2	3	4
• Listen to what each other says.	1	2	3	4
• Avoid put-downs.	1	2	3	4
• Include each other in games and working groups.	1	2	3	4
• Treat each other's cultural traditions with respect.	1	2	3	4

My major strength in following these norms is:

_____

One normative behavior I would like to strengthen is:

_____

My strategy for strengthening it is: _____

I will monitor my efforts for five days by evaluating the refinement and improvement of this normative behavior on the same 4-point scale.

Day one: 1   2   3   4   Day four: 1   2   3   4

Day two: 1   2   3   4   Day five: 1   2   3   4

Day three: 1   2   3   4

Evidence that I have strengthened this behavior: _____

_____

One strategy I can use to keep it strong: _____

_____

Provide Opportunities for Students To Demonstrate Learning in Diverse Ways

In addition to helping students internalize behavioral habits that support high levels of learning, focus on the ways in which students differ.

Start by recognizing that all learners enter your classroom with a constellation of readiness levels, learning profiles, and interests that influence how they learn. Assess and use these differences to plan and deliver instruction that promotes growth. Research by Carol Ann Tomlinson and other noted experts and practitioners shed light on three basic factors that you can mine to provide students with diverse ways of demonstrating learning.

Student Readiness
Learning Profile
Student Interest

Think of these basic factors as ways to understand student needs as you plan instruction that enables each student to demonstrate learning.

Differentiation Factor #1: Student Readiness

Simply stated, readiness is a student's current status to work with and master a particular set of new knowledge, concepts, or skills. While some students come to you ready to learn essential knowledge and skills in their grade level curriculum, others may lag behind and need extra support. A hidden element may be students who do such excellent work that they are not extending their knowledge and skills. Here's an example from a conversation with a college freshman:

In high school, I displayed my writing ability with ease but I haven't developed it further, so I yearn for challenges that will make me dig deep down to stretch my capacity.

Make **tiered instruction** and **tiered assignments** part of your instructional design. Not only will they help you confirm and define each student's readiness for the work ahead, but also they provide pathways of least resistance (and greatest facility) for them.

Tiered instruction often relies on flexible grouping so that students can approach the same concepts and skills but at differing levels of difficulty, abstractness, and rigor depending on their readiness. In this way, you can scaffold instruction to these readiness levels and provide support as needed by each group.

To organize flexible groups, start by identifying the concept(s) and skill(s) from the approved curriculum that are the desired outcome for the unit of study or individual lesson. Next, determine readiness levels of students by administering either formal pre-formative assessments for a standard or unit, or else a brief formative assessment at the outset or end of a lesson. Then use assessment data to plan and deliver tiered instruction that is adjusted for students' various readiness levels. Keep guidelines like these in mind as you organize your students into flexible instructional groups:

Three Steps in Organizing Flexible Groups

1. **Pre-Assess:** Design a short pre-assessment at the outset of a lesson to identify variations in students' levels of understanding in relation to the new concept or skill to be learned. Use the data to form your groups. Tailor your delivery by scaffolding instruction to the various readiness levels. For example, one group may simply need a short explanation at grade level and then can work independently to practice concepts and skills while another group may be ready for instruction on concepts and skills beyond grade level accompanied by more challenging tasks for independent practice. Still another group may require more foundational work to

continued on next page

prepare them to learn the new concept or skill followed by independent practice with simpler tasks.

2. **Devise Diverse Instruction:** For each group (see examples in #1) you may conduct a different number of instructional sessions. For example, one group may need two sessions if they have not mastered pre-requisite skills—one session to pre-teach missing pre-requisites, one session to move into the skill focus of the lesson. For students who have already mastered the concept or skill, you might move them quickly into more complex practice.

3. **Combine Pre-Assessment with Embedded Assessment:** Devise a pre-assessment for the very beginning of the lesson (this can be a brief activity that requires each student to respond). Briefly teach the new concept/skill to the whole group at that level while including an embedded formative assessment as you proceed in order to gauge progress. Use that data to move students who are ready into independent practice. Re-teach the concept as necessary to students who do not yet understand. If possible, administer yet another embedded assessment to determine those who have achieved mastery and identify the needs of students who have not. Re-teach the concept in a way that is adjusted to the needs of the remaining students. Release students to independent practice as they demonstrate mastery.[22]

A critical step in this process is to provide **tiered assignments**—opportunities for students to practice or demonstrate mastery of the same concepts and skills at differing levels of complexity. **Tiered assignments** increase the likelihood that students will develop core content and skills for their grade level while maximizing the challenge by encouraging them to stretch beyond their comfort levels yet within their capacities for success. And if you are completely successful, you help students not only to learn, but also to develop habits of persistence, curiosity, and a willingness to take intellectual risks.[19]

To create effective tiered assignments, begin by identifying the learning outcome and then by assessing students to find their levels of readiness. Researcher Carol Ann Tomlinson suggests steps like these:

Steps in Devising Tiered Assignments

1. Identify the desired learning outcomes (concepts and skills) that students should master. Develop learning tasks that address those.

2. Assess range of readiness levels or reflect on students' learning profiles and/or interests.

3. Create an activity that offers students …
   a. high levels of interest,
   b. high level of quality, and
   c. challenge in using key skill(s) to understand important ideas.

4. Place the activity on the appropriate level of complexity.

5. Clone the activity along the ladder of complexity as needed to ensure challenge and success for all students.

6. Place each student's name on the ladder beside the level of complexity for which each is ready. (See Examples #1 and #2, which follow.)

Coming Up: Following are two examples of Tiered Assignments.

#1 On the facing page is a Tiered Assignment at the primary grade level.

#2 Following the primary example is one at an upper level.

Example 1: Tiered Assignments for Primary Level		
Intended Learning Outcome: *Students will compare and contrast characters in two stories.*		
Ladder of Complexity	**Activities**	**Students Assigned to that Level**
High skill complexity	Use a Venn Diagram to compare the differences and similarities in the role played by the author, Margie Palatini, with the role played by the illustrator, Howard Fine, in showing the characteristics of the pigs in *Piggie Pie*.	Jared, Juanita, Aadila
Middle skill complexity	Use a Venn Diagram to compare the pigs in the *Three Little Pigs* with the pigs in *Piggie Pie* by Marjorie Palatini.	Jose, Sophia, Daniel, Andrea, George, Franco, Manuel, Natalie...
Low-skill complexity	**Make two Lists:** • 3 ways the pigs in *Piggie Pie* are different from the pigs in the *Three Little Pigs*. • 3 ways the pigs in *Piggie Pie* are the same as in the *Three Little Pigs*.	Camille, Joan, Anthony

Example 2: Tiered Assignments for Secondary Level		
Learning Outcome: *Students will explain how slavery and other geographic, social, economic, and political differences between the North and South led to the Civil War.*		
Ladder of Complexity	**Activities**	**Students Assigned to that Level**
High skill complexity	• Review the major causes, events, results of the Revolutionary War and the Civil War. • Work in groups of four to formulate a theory of war and support it with reasons and facts derived from multiple sources such as text, historical news articles, diaries, videos, resources from an internet search, etc. • Make a T-chart of the causes of the Civil War and the Revolutionary War. • Identify major events of the Revolutionary War and Civil War. • Identify the costs and benefits of each. • Prepare a formal presentation of your theory to the class.	Deborah, Sterling, Sue, Thuyen, Olaf

continued on next page

Middle High skill complexity	**Work in Triads:** • On chart paper, sketch a political cartoon that promotes the South's cause for seceding from the Union or the Union's case for not allowing them to secede. • Write an editorial that makes the case for the side you selected, supporting your stance with reasoning and evidence.	Dow, Lynette, Archer, Maria, Chevy, Joan, Adrienne, Le, Brian, Haadee, Charles…
Middle skill complexity	• In Triads, discuss ways in which the abolitionist movement increased tensions between the North and South. List in order of seriousness. • Write a paragraph that explains the ways the abolitionist movement increased tensions between the North and South.	Lissa, Loren, Sebastian, Chau, Sofia, Valeria, Christyn, Samuel, Ayser, Hans…
Low-skill complexity	Read the text. • List 5 cultural differences between the North & South. • List 4 economic differences between the North and South. • Share your thinking with a partner.	Jan, Justin, Joshua, Jenny…

You can structure Tiered Assignments in a variety of ways. **Tiering by *complexity*** means providing learners with the same assignment with varying levels of difficulty that address their readiness levels. **Tiering by *process*** provides students with the choice of which processes they will use to achieve similar outcomes. **Tiering by *product*** provides learners opportunities to hone skills or to operate in their preferred learning styles. For instance, one group may dramatize a historical event, another group might write a newspaper article about it, while another group may make a political cartoon or a cartoon strip about the event. You can also **Tier by *varying resources*** based on their levels of difficulty, medium, or topics. For example, some students may use journal articles, others may use digital resources, while others might use visual representations of the knowledge, such as cartoon books, videos, diagrams, illustrations, and so forth.

Differentiation Factor #2: Learning Profile (Learning Modalities)

Each student's learning profile—gender, culture, intelligence preferences, learning styles (modalities)—gives enormous insight into how s/he learns best. For instance, when a student learns through a preferred style (kinesthetic, visual, auditory, etc.) s/he uses less energy to process, thus having more energy to devote to remembering, comprehending, and applying new learning.

Kinesthetic learners learn best through movement, experimentation with objects, and hands-on manipulatives. Himmele and Himmele recommend that teachers actively engage students in learning that involves movement. The possibilities for introducing movement are endless. Here are a few:

> ***Mix and Mingle*** is one simple strategy for introducing movement. For example, a teacher may use mix and mingle to have students discuss issues relevant to the lesson such as this: *Explain to another person the reasoning processes you used to solve the story problem.* Or this: *Share with another student the evidence you found that geese work together.* While the teacher says *Mix, mix, mix...,* students move

around the room. When the teacher says *mingle*, students stop moving and talk with a person standing next to them. After a suitable interval, the teacher instructs students to *mix*, at which point they stop talking and move around the room. At the signal of *mingle*, they stop moving and talk with a new partner. After three or more times, not only do students get to move, but by sharing their thinking or learning with another person, they deepen and broaden their understanding of new learning.

In ***Learning new vocabulary words***, for instance, an elementary teacher might introduce the new vocabulary word and give students a movement that demonstrates its meaning. For example, for the meaning of the word *flexible*, students may contort their body in strange ways. Or for words with more than one meaning, such as *beat*, the teacher may give students a movement for each meaning such as clapping to a certain beat or making whipping motions to stir up an egg, or making the victory sign to symbolize defeating another person or team in a competition.

Dramatizing an event or a concept engages kinesthetic learners actively. For example, students can dramatize the contrasting movement of water molecules in a liquid state and in a gaseous state. Or they can create movement that demonstrates the four stages of the life cycle of a butterfly. Students can also dramatize an historical event such as the Boston Tea Party or the narrative of a story. To dramatize well, students must dig deeply to understand the concept or historical event well enough to transform that understanding into action.

Auditory learners learn best through verbal instruction and talking about what they've learned. They like rhymes and chants and enjoy background music while they study. These students enjoy small group or whole group discussions of ideas and concepts.[19] You can find myriad ways to organize for student-to-student interaction around new concepts and skills. Here are some that work well with a range of students:

> ***Three-minute Pause:*** Stop at any time during direct instruction or discussion to give groups or teams three minutes to review what has been covered. Follow by asking questions that clarify or extend.

> ***Team-Pair-Solo:*** Students solve problems or challenges first as a team, then with a partner, and finally on their own. Such a progression builds skills and independence.

> ***Number Heads Together:*** Give a number to each group member in each group. Pose a problem for all members to discuss and solve. Call a number and that student is responsible for sharing for the group.

> ***Rimes and chants:*** Researcher Patricia Cunningham offers a strategy for working with onset (the initial sound in a word) and rime (the string of letters that follow the onset) to help students use the base of one word (rime) to decode new words as they change the initial consonant, digraph, or blend (onset). To set this up, you can put a card with a rime, such as "ap" on it on a word chart. For the rime "ap," the following consonants could be used to make new words: c, t, l, m, n, r, s, z. Students would begin the chant with just the rime and then make new words by adding different onsets. The teacher changes the onsets to make new words using this chant:

> *Give me an "a," add a "p," What have you got? ap*
> *Add a "c." What have we got? cap!*
> *Take off the "c" (remove the c). What have we got? ap!*
> *Add an "l" (place an l in front of ap). What have*
> *we got? lap!*

> You can repeat this process for every onset that you have displayed.

Visual learners enjoy seeing or creating visual representations of new knowledge or concepts. Typically, they like to take notes and enhance them with doodles. These learners prefer having knowledge and skills presented to them visually and in short snatches. Visual learners enjoy using brightly colored highlighters to highlight important points in a text. A few strategies from Himmele's and Himmele's work with active engagement provide useful ways to engage these learners in their preferred mode. The first strategy is for students to make a quick sketch that illustrates a new concept or skill.[9]

> **Quick Draw**s are opportunities for students to demonstrate their understanding of an abstract term or concept by representing it in a drawing and can be used with almost any age group, from young children through adults with any content area. First, select a "big idea" or major concept within your lesson. Ask students to reflect on the meaning of the concept and to create a visual image that represents that concept (allow approximately three to five minutes). Then ask students to share and explain their image with a partner, in a small group.

> **Picture Notes** provide time for students to stop and process what they have learned and to enhance written notes, not to replace them. At selected junctures in the lesson, pause for students to make a sketch that illustrates what they have learned from that section. For example, in a study of weather, ask students to sketch the first of three types of cloud formations, or in a study of the American Revolution, ask students to visually represent three major disagreements colonists had with England.

> **Visual Problem Solving** works especially well in mathematics. Students first use close reading strategies to read and reread a story problem while using color to highlight important information/facts, the question itself, and math vocabulary that they don't understand. They also

cross out unimportant information, identify hidden questions, and predict operations that will reach a solution. The key is to have students diagram or sketch a visual representation of the problem in order to gain a clearer understanding of the problem and to predict more closely what the answer will be.[14]

Differentiation Factor #3: Student Interest

Every student is, or can become, interested in something. Allowing students to learn essential concepts and skills through their interests introduces passion into the learning process.[19,20] A key ingredient in student interest is **choice**. Simply put, students learn more and retain it longer when they get to choose what they learn, to choose how to learn it, and to choose how to demonstrate what they learn.[12]

In a study of two groups of ballet students (all starting at the same skill level) during a day-long lesson about "moves" and "positions" in their dance, one group was allowed to choose their video demonstrations while the other did not choose but were assigned their video demonstrations. An assessment at the end of the day revealed that, while both groups progressed, the choice group made significantly greater progress and scored higher on measures of self-efficacy and happiness. Conclusion: Giving students voice in their education develops a greater sense of themselves as agents in their own learning. They develop more intrinsic motivation to learn.[10,12]

Further research tells us that choice must be scaffolded in ways that ensure students get the optimal benefits. For example, if students are given too many choices (30 choices versus 5-6), researchers found diminishing returns.[16] Here are some guidelines about choice that research suggests:

Facilitate Student Interest through Choice

1. Establish the learning outcomes (concepts and/or skills) students should work with.

2. Design options that cause students to understand the focus concepts and develop targeted skills.

3. Avoid overwhelming students with too many choices:
   a. Give only a few choices for less experienced learners.
   b. Start every student out with a few choices and gradually introduce more choices up to 4-6, not more than nine.

4. Differentiate the number of choices, complexity of choices, and level of support you provide learners based on their degree of self-direction, readiness levels, learning profile, interests, and so forth.

Experts and savvy practitioners have found endless ways to differentiate learning through choice.

One of these ways is a form of **Tic-Tac-Toe** that uses the format of an old game children play to structure learner choices.

In the example that follows, a teacher has identified the essential concept(s) and skill(s) for students to learn and then designed a menu of activities that engage students in learning them. [19,20]

In this example of a Tic-Tac-Toe adapted from Carol Ann Tomlinson's work, notice that a format of nine cells placed in three rows and three columns offers students numerous choices suitable for a wide variety of student interests and competencies:

CHOOSE YOUR TASK

Instructions: For the famous American whose biography you have read, select one activity from each horizontal row to help you think about his or her life.

Learning Outcome: *I can read and comprehend a biography of an individual who contributed greatly to America. This means I can...*

- identify major challenges this individual faced.
- highlight major contributions.
- compare and contrast my life with his/her life.

Famous American	Individual: Use a graphic organizer to compare and contrast yourself with the American you studied.	Write a biopoem for you and the American you studied to show how you are alike and different.	Describe a problem you face and how you will solve it. Describe how the American you studied might solve that same problem.
Challenges Faced	Make a collage that shows the challenges your famous American faced in his/her life.	Create a political cartoon that illustrates the challenges with which this American struggled.	Identify four of the greatest challenges faced by your character and incorporate them into a rap.
Contributions to Society	Partner: Draw a cartoon strip that highlights the important contributions this American made to our society.	Partner: Conduct an interview with the American you studied to discover what s/he contributed to society and what lessons s/he learned.	Select the major contributions your American made to society and write a journal article that introduces him/her as the *Person of the Year.*

RAFT activities provide differentiation for students by readiness, interest, and learning profile. RAFT takes its name from the first letters of four words: Role, Audience, Format, and Topic. With a RAFT activity, all students study the same topic, one that gets at the core of essential concepts and skills. Each student chooses a role to play and chooses the audience and the format by which to demonstrate learning and development. While these four components work together, each contributes uniquely to learning benefits for students:

1. **R**ole. This component challenges students to write from a perspective that may be different than their own, which causes them to move outside themselves, develop a broader understanding, and develop greater flexibility in their ability to express themselves through writing.

2. **A**udience. Most students write to one audience: the teacher. By varying the audience to whom the students address their thinking, they choose their writer's voice, reasoning, rationale, and information/facts more strategically.

3. **F**ormat. By writing from differing formats, students stretch their writing prowess into diverse formats such as essays, explanations, opinion/argumentation, narrative, and so forth.

4. **T**opic. The topic is simply the content about which students will be writing. Starting with the topic is helpful because it allows you to relate it to the learning outcomes you wish students to master or deepen.[19;20]

Here is an example of a RAFT activity designed for secondary students in a United States History II course to invite students to delve deeply into social changes that occurred in the 20th century because of the Civil Rights Movement. Notice how all the topics are related to the stated Learning Objectives and the Success Criteria.

CHOOSE YOUR ROLE

Learning Objective: *I can demonstrate understanding of the social changes that were sought by, and resulted from, the Civil Rights Movement.*

Success Criteria: Presentation, demonstrations of...

- objectives held by various groups.
- strategies various groups used to achieve desired outcomes.
- effectiveness of various strategies.
- degree to which racial and ethnic minorities, women, American Indians, and other marginalized groups have achieved objectives of the Civil Rights Movement.

Roll	Audience	Format	Topic
Columnist, *The New York Times*	Readers of *The New York Times*	Op-Ed Column expressing a strong informed opinion	Craft a strong informed opinion of the objectives of Civil Rights Movement to end public segregation.
Civil Rights Lawyer	Supreme Court	Opening Statement	Convince judges that the state-sanctioned segregation of public schools is a violation of the Equal Protection Clause under the 14th amendment and is therefore unconstitutional.
African American forced to sit in rear section on a bus	Postcrity	Diary Entry	Demonstrate the injustice of "separate but equal" doctrine from a personal perspective.

continued on next page

Documentary Film Maker	American Public	Script	Portray the key events in the Civil Rights struggle to achieve full equality.

Learning Menus offer students opportunities to select and pursue in-depth aspects of core concepts and skills that pique their interest, while also ensuring that they master essentials from the curriculum learning standard.[20] Give the learning menu to students mid-way through a unit at a point where students will have acquired requisite knowledge and skills to complete the tasks on the menu independently. Begin by identifying the desired Learning Outcomes and Success Criteria. Then develop a range of activities that engage students in exploring and applying their learning in a variety of ways. In the learning menu example that follows, notice how the learning activities address a variety of learning styles:

CHOOSE YOUR TASK

Two Outcomes:
- *I can identify the factors that brought people to the American West.*
- *I can analyze the settlement of the American West.*

Success Criteria: *I will know I have achieved these outcomes when I can...*
- present reasons why people came to the West, including farmers, ranchers, miners, American Indian nations, immigrants, and so forth.

- assess the impact of the railroad on western development.

- determine the reasons that motivated groups involved in conflicts that developed during the settlement of the West, including farmers, ranchers, miners, American Indian nations, immigrants, and so forth.

- analyze the conflicts with the American Indian nations.

---

continued on next page

Appetizer	**Select two of the resources provided to gather additional information:**
	
	• Videos book-marked on the Web that detail the reasons people moved to the American West.
	
	• Articles from the Smithsonian Institute on these topics:
	  – Conflicts among the groups that settled the West.
	  – Costs and benefits of expanding the railroad to the American West.
	  – Analysis of the effects of Westward Expansion on American Indian nations in the American West.
	  – One of the chapters marked in two books on the history of the settlement of the American West.
	  – A copy of an actual journal kept by one of the builders of the railroad.

Main Course	**Complete each learning activity:** • For one of the information sources you studied, keep a three-column multi-entry journal in which you (a) record key concepts, (b) reflect on why you think each concept/event is important, and (c) hypothesize what a historical expert on that topic might say to you. • From the point of view of a cattle rancher, write an editorial that persuades an audience to the rancher's opinion about farmers settling in their western areas. • As a social scientist, write a journal article that analyzes, from a historical perspective, the reasons various people moved to the American West and what the costs and benefits were. Include in that analysis the expansion of the railroad to the West. • Use a graphic organizer to compare and contrast the American Indian nations with one of the groups that settled the American West.

continued on next page

Dessert	**Select at least one of these options:**
	• Draw a political cartoon that gives a perspective from one of the groups involved in the conflicts in the settlement of the American West.
	• With another person, dramatize an argument that might take place between a rancher and a farmer.
	• Draw a serious cartoon strip that details the unintended consequences of the westward expansion for the American Indian nations.
	• Write a historical poem or rap that details the history of one group's settlement of the West.
	• Choreograph and perform an interpretive dance depicting one group's experience in moving to and settling the West, and explain the significance of various aspects of the dance.
	• Write one week of daily journal entries of one settler's experience living in the West. Base your entries on actual evidence.
	• Design a series of pictographs that a member of one American Indian nation might draw to communicate his or her experiences with peoples who settled the West. Base these pictographs on actual events and effects.

To set students up to succeed academically in an environment offering choice, start at the beginning of the year to prepare students systematically to exercise autonomy in making academic choices while producing high quality results. In addition to teaching behavioral habits that support independent learning, you can prepare students academically through choice in a few more ways:

Additional Hints for Using Choice

- Systematically teach study skills that equip your students to access and capture information from a variety of primary and secondary resource materials.

- Promote students' ability to use higher levels of cognitive thought to process and generate new knowledge.

- Teach and nurture reasoning processes.

- Help students develop habits of mind such as persisting, thinking flexibly, taking responsible risks, etc.

- Teach students to read closely and fully respond to the directions to the activities they choose.

- Provide rubrics that students can use to self-reflect and to improve the quality of their efforts.

- At the beginning of the year, incorporate skills that students acquired in previous years into the choice activities you design.

- As your students develop new skills, incorporate them into your choice activities.

Link Effort and Achievement To Foster Student Perseverance

Can you teach perseverance to your students, or to anyone for that matter? Angela Duckworth, Associate Professor of Psychology at the University of Pennsylvania, believes that the answer is "Yes," as follows:

> ...*some people are, in general, more persistent and passionate about long-term goals. Compared to their less gritty peers, these individuals are more resilient in the face of adversity, bouncing back after failure and disappointment and otherwise staying the course even when progress is not obvious. Second, grit predicts success. Grit is not the only determinant of success—opportunity and talent matter, too. But on average, grittier individuals are more successful than others, particularly in very challenging situations.*

So, can we intentionally cultivate grit in our children, in our employees, in ourselves? Relative to many other scholarly traditions, the science of behavior change is in its infancy. Still, we know enough, I think, to answer that question in the affirmative. Can perseverance be taught? Yes. Do we know how? More and more—though, of course, there is much to be discovered.[3]

Researchers also have found that students who are taught about the relationship between effort and achievement increase their achievement more than students who are taught techniques for time management and comprehension of new material.

And because research also tells us that students generally contribute their success or failure to one of these four causes:

- Ability
- Effort
- Other people
- Luck

then it stands to reason that we can foster student perseverance by teaching them how to link effort with achievement. So how might you do that?

One way is to examine with students exactly what we mean by "effort" since there is not much you can do or say about ability, other people, and dumb luck. You can take time with students to address "effort" as a personal characteristic or quality. Fashion a process of examining "effort" and ask students to define it, to look for examples of it, to demonstrate it, and ultimately to practice it. The immediate advantage of this exercise is to alert students to your own awareness of their "effort" and to alert them to your respect for "effort." The process you follow with them will reinforce this perception and possibly will introduce students to a deeper understanding of "effort" and its benefits. Here is a simple process, or set of steps, that you might follow:

Process for Exploring "Effort"

1. <u>Define:</u> What does effort look like/sound like?
2. <u>Demo:</u> Demonstrate the wrong way and the right way.
3. <u>Practice</u> the right way.
4. <u>Refine:</u> Track the relationship between effort and achievement.

Another way is to develop visual prompts in your classroom that address "effort" and perseverance. You might develop first-person statements like these during the course of your process for exploring "effort" or you might simply post them for discussion as needed. Here are some examples:

What is Effort? (first grade example)

I keep trying even when I want to stop.

I think hard of more than one way I can do my work.

I say "I think I can" to myself.

I ask for help after I have tried really hard.

What is Perseverance? (high school example)

When I'm not quite sure what to do, I think through my options and keep working.

I am not hesitant to do work more than once. I value refining.

I stop during my work and reflect if I am doing my best work.

I ask for help after I have made at least three attempts.

I monitor the link between my effort and my achievement.

Self-tracking may be one of the strongest approaches to building a connection between effort and accomplishment. You can help students do this by constructing a tracking device for certain tasks for which they are responsible. While a device like this works on so many levels (assignment reminders, self-reflection, etc.) it also helps focus each student on his or her effort. And "effort" is the key to perseverance—more than ability, more than other people, more than dumb luck. Here's a format you might use:

My Weekly Tracking Chart					
Date	Assignment	My Grade	My effort (1 low - 4 high)	I'm glad that I...	I need to...
9/5	Self-Start	B	3		
9/7	Essay: Good vs Bad	C	1		
9/9	Source Examination	D	1		
9/14	Google Page	A	4		

Once students have created data, they are able to reflect and to infer that their effort leads to good grades and to success generally. And you can always dig into your bag of student engagement strategies for just the right cueing statements. Here are a few:

Cueing for Perseverance	
First-Person Cueing	Third-Person Cueing
When I'm not quite sure what to do, I think through my options and keep working.	I can see you trying different options, which is a great example of perseverance.
I am not hesitant to do work more than once. I value refining.	Thank you for jumping right in to refine your work. This effort will really pay off for you.

Help Students Develop Meta-Cognitive Skills

Self knowledge (metacognition) can take one a long way because it can open doors to such things as rational thinking and sound decision-making. Among the many opportunities that you have to enrich your students is the opportunity to help each one develop meta-cognitively.

Perhaps Shakespeare said it best: "To thine own self be true, and [good things] shall follow as the night the day."

Centuries later, education researchers concur about the value of self knowledge, or self awareness. Some point to the disadvantages of poor meta-cognition. For instance, an overly confident student may make incorrect choices due to a shallow understanding of information. Conversely, an under-performing student may not recognize his or hew own power, but once recognized and harnessed, latent abilities blossom to move that student forward. [1,2,3,4]

The irony here is that the same is true for teachers. If you think meta-cognitively about your strengths as a teacher—your concern for each student, for instance, or your insights into a student's needs and abilities—you are moving forward toward developing meta-cognitive skills for others, specifically your students. Think of it as a self-fulfilling prophesy.

So what techniques can you employ? Here are four kinds, although no limit exists to the possibilities you can find to growing your students' self-awareness and helping them apply it.

Meta Technique # One: Teach Students To Self-Regulate.
Especially with very young children, it makes sense to teach such things as self-starting behaviors because this type of practice, by its very nature, requires students to think about what they're doing physically and mentally. You are helping them build intrinsic skills through self-awareness.

The meta-cognitive aspect of self-regulating includes each student's internal thoughts and feelings about the process you put before him. For instance, if you are teaching your expectations for Bell Ringer Daily Activities, a common type of self-starter, you might ask students to envision themselves as they enter class and take their seats. Creating a "Looks Like / Sounds Like" chart with students requires them to think about what they "look like" and what they "sound like" as they start class. Here are four typical steps in teaching a self-starter:

Step 1: Describe. Tell students what you expect by describing the procedure. Tell them why it is important and why they will benefit from developing such a habit. Ask volunteers if they have followed such a procedure in the past. Then develop a visual or graphic like a Looks Like / Sounds Like chart. If really necessary, have children copy the graphic or make copies for them. Keep it posted in the room.

Step 2: Demonstrate. Ask two students to role play. Have them demonstrate the procedure while others watch. Have them demonstrate the wrong way and then the right way. After each demonstration, debrief by referring to a graphic like a Looks Like/ Sounds Like chart. (K teachers! You should be the one to do the demo.)

Step 3: Practice. Give a mock simulation. For instance, have students leave and re-enter the classroom to show how they will recognize and begin a bell-ringer activity.

Step 4: Maintain and Re-Direct. Maintain the habit by offering positive reminders. Verbally support work well done. "Thank you, Loren, for starting your bell-ringer before the bell has rung." Use your Looks Like / Sounds Like graphic to remind yourself of specific cues. As necessary, repeat Steps 2 and 3 with those who seem to "forget" the procedure during the year. Remember: Step 4 never ends!

If any of your students don't yet self-regulate successfully, you may have very important fundamental work to do in order to help them develop meta-cognitive skills. It's also possible that only a few of your students have yet to acquire self-regulation; if so, you may need to work on this skill with them separately or in a group.

By teaching students to self-regulate, or to heighten their skills at self-regulating, you are helping them gain independence, and researchers tell us that gaining independence leads to increasing levels of performance.

Meta Technique # Two: Teach Students To Self-Analyze.
When you teach your students a habit (e.g., in steps 1 and 2 above), you are encouraging them to self-analyze (e.g., creating a graphic together or role-playing). That's a good start, but you can go much further. Deeper self-analysis requires data and evidence. Your students have the ability to rate themselves at various tasks that you identify for them (e.g., in a self-assessment form after a week of Bell Ringers), and you have the opportunity to guide the data that they collect so that their data becomes evidence of their performance—both the good and the bad.

It stands to reason that the effort it takes for each student to externalize what he or she knows internally is an effort that creates or strengthens a mental connection—a pathway for the free flow of self awareness. Sometimes your students will access good news about their thoughts and behavior, and sometimes not so much. At the ready, however, you have the opportunity to help your student put that information to constructive use, which is why it's always best for you to focus on the positive aspects of each student's self-analysis data.

Here's an example of an elementary level student self-assessment form. Notice that each student's meta-cognitive activity is two-fold: (1) to rate himself by reflecting on past performance, and (2) to self-analyze by externalizing each rating:

My Name_____ Today's Date _____

How Well Do I Perform on my Bell Ringer Activity?

1 = Poor   2 = Fair   3 = Very Well   4 = Extremely Well

	My Rating
I enter the classroom quietly every day.	
Why I gave myself this rating:	
I put my stuff away immediately.	
Why I gave myself this rating:	
I get the required materials out.	
Why I gave myself this rating:	
I begin work immediately.	
Why I gave myself this rating:	
I continue to work without being distracted.	
Why I gave myself this rating:	

And here's an example of a self-assessment form from secondary. Notice this time that each group of ratings leads to two different aspects of self-analysis: (1) reflecting on and analyzing past performance, and (2) projecting future performance, or improvement:

Student Self-Assessment of a Long-Term Project

Name_____Class:_____Date _____

	Poor	Avg.	Good	Excel
Academic Criteria				
• Topic well-researched				
• Broad range of resources used				
• Information written in my own words				
• Multiple viewpoints represented				

continued on next page

What did I do best?				
What can I strengthen?				
Life Skills	**Poor**	**Avg.**	**Good**	**Excel**
• My efforts were focused.				
• My time was used wisely.				
• My work ethic was good.				
• I avoided distracting others.				
What did I do best?				
What can I strengthen?				

Meta Technique # Three: Teach Students To Track and Self-Project. A most constructive aspect of building students' meta-cognitive skills is leading them to project future performance based on what they perceive about their current performance. If you have students track themselves—on projects, assignments, and other kinds of performance—you can lead them deeper, meta-cognitively. For instance, by asking them to make inferences and judgments about their performance, you can take them a step further by asking them to envision desirable _changes_ in their performance.

Self-tracking may be one of the strongest approaches to building a connection between effort, accomplishment, and future progress. Here is an example of a tracking device for certain tasks:

My Weekly Tracking Chart					
Date	Assignment	My Grade	My Effort (1 low – 4 high)	I'm glad that I...	I need to...
9/5	Self-Start	B	3		
9/7	Essay: Good vs Bad	C	1		
9/9	Source Examination	D	1		
9/14	Google Page	A	4		

Meta Technique # Four: Employ Self-Reflective Tactics in Real Time. Encourage students to reflect on their own skills and knowledge as they work. Help them keep their strengths in mind as they engage with new concepts and attempt to acquire new skills. Be mindful of questions you can ask—and questions that you can prompt students to ask of themselves—during all phases of their endeavor. Here are a few examples:

As students approach a task, have each one of them ask self-reflective questions. You can present such questions in the specific context of the task, naturally, but generally the questions will look like this: *What do I already know about this? What do I need to learn? Where can I start? What can I do first? Second? Who can I consult with to check if I'm on the right track?*

As students dive into a task, shape questions more specific than generic ones like *Am I getting anywhere?* Instead, ask more specific ones like *What information have I found that I think is useful? What information may not help? Do I need to change direction in some way? What additional information will help me? Who can I consult with to help me decide on my progress and direction?*

And as students go deeper into a task, as they actually make progress, you can support their meta-cognitive engines with questions like these: *What work so far should I review and re-evaluate? What am I still missing? How can I expand, develop, or augment the results I have achieved? Who can I consult with to help me identify needs that remain?*

And context is quite important for you to consider so that you can sharpen the meta-cognitive questions you present for students. For instance, if students are collecting data from history sources that they are reading, consider asking them to take notes in ways that suit the way each student thinks. Before they begin reading and taking notes, ask them to create a note-taking diagram with three or four distinct areas on it. Have them label each of the note-taking areas and see what they come up with. For instance, a student with "Interpersonal Intelligence"[5] may label one area "People Who Made a Difference."

On the other hand, to approach a writing assignment like an essay or research paper, you might ask students to diagram their ideas. One visual learner might draw a pyramid and place the central idea at the top and supporting ideas and details beneath in some schematic way.

The point is simply this: Ask leading questions—questions that lead students into thoughts of their personal ways of thinking and feeling—and connect those questions to the concepts and contexts of the task at hand.

Consult Experts

1. Cunningham, P. *Phonics They Use: Words for Reading and Writing* (7th Edition). Boston, MA: Pearson, 2017.

2. Deal, T. E. and Peterson, K. D. *Shaping School Culture: Pitfalls, Paradoxes, and Promises* (2nd Edition). San Francisco, CA: Jossey-Bass, 2009.

3. Duckworth, A. "Grit: The Power of Passion and Perseverance." *Ted Talks*. New York, NY, April 2013. Lecture.

4. Forlini, G., Williams, E., and Brinkman, A. *Class Acts: Your Guide To Activate Learning* (3rd Edition). Bronxville, NY: Lavender Hill Press, 2016.

5. Goodwin, B. "Giving Students Meaningful Work." *Educational Leadership.* 68(1), September 2010.

6. Gregory, G. H. and Chapman, C. *Differentiated Instructional Strategies: One Size Doesn't Fit All.* Thousand Oaks, CA: Corwin Press, Inc., 2002.

7. Hattie, J. and Timperley, H. "The Power of Feedback." *Review of Educational Research*, 77(1), 2007.

8. Hattie, J. *Visible Learning for Teachers: Maximizing Impact on Learning.* New York, NY: Routledge, 2012.

9. Himmele, P. and Himmele, W. *Total Participation Techniques: Making Every Student an Active Learner.* Alexandria, VA: Association for Supervision and Curriculum Development, 2011.

10. Kageyama, N. "How (and Why) Giving Students Choices, Can Dramatically Improve Learning." *The Bulletproof Musician.* https://bulletproofmusician.com/giving-students-choices-can-dramatically-improve-learning/. online

11. Kounin, J. *Discipline and Group Management in Classrooms.* New York, NY: Holt, Rinehart and Winston, 1971.

12. Lemos, A., Wulf, G., Lewthwaite, R., and Chiviacowsky, S. "Autonomy Support Enhances Performance Expect-ancies, Positive Affect, and Motor Learning." *Psychology of Sport and Exercise.* July 31, 2017.

13. McCarthy, J. "Establish A Culture of Student Voice." *Edutopia.* www.edutopia.org/blog/establishing-culture-of-student-voice-john-mccarthy. 2015. online

14. Meyer, K. "Making Meaning in Mathematics Problem-Solving Using the Reciprocal Teaching Approach. "*Literacy Learning: The Middle Years*. 22 (2), June 2014.

15. Paul, R. and Elder, L. "Foundation for Critical Thinking." 1997. www.criticalthinking.org. online

16. Patall, E., Cooper, H., and Robinson, J. C. "The Effects of Choice on Intrinsic Motivation and Related Outcomes: A Meta-Analysis of Research Findings." *Psychological Bulletin*, 134 (2), 2007.

17. Peterson, K. D. and Deal, T. E. *The Shaping School Culture Fieldbook*. San Francisco, CA: Josey-Bass, 2002.

18. Shute, V. J. *Focus on Formative Feedback*. Princeton, NJ: Educational Testing Service, 2007.

19. Tomlinson, C. A. and Eidson, C. C. *Differentiation in Practice: A Resource Guide for Differentiating Curriculum*. Alexandria, VA: Association for Supervision and Curriculum Development, 2003.

20. Tomlinson, C. A. *Fulfilling the Promise of the Differentiated Classroom*. Alexandria, VA: ASCD, 2003.

21. Van Overwalle, F. and De Metsenaere, M. "The Effects of Attribution-Based Intervention and Study Strategy Training on Academic Achievement in College Freshmen." *British Journal of Educational Psychology* 60, 1990.

22. Wiliam, D. *Embedded Formative Assessment*. Bloomington, IN: Solution Tree Press, 2011.

Self-Assess: Providing Students with Multiple Ways To Demonstrate Learning

For each element, self-assess using the following 1-4 scale:

1. **Missing (I need to do this)**
2. **Attempted (I try to do this, but I am not successful)**
3. **Apparent (I do this well, but I don't do it consistently. When I do it, it works!)**
4. **Well Done (I do this consistently and appropriately)**

Part I: Establish an Inclusive Environment that Supports High Levels of Diverse Learning

Teach 3-4 Critical Behavioral Habits   1 2 3 4
At the beginning of the school year, I teach students 3-4 critical behavioral habits that support high levels of learning.

Support Students To Internalize Critical Habits   1 2 3 4
I use effective feedback (specific positive cueing) to motivate and support students to internalize the 3-4 critical behavioral habits.

Support Students To Internalize Critical Habits   1 2 3 4
I use physical and visual proximity strategically to establish a "felt presence" with my students and position myself to intervene at the onset of disruptive behaviors before they ripple through the class.

Cultivate an Inclusive Learning Culture   1 2 3 4
I work with my students systematically to develop norms, attitudes, and dispositions that foster inclusion.

Part II: Provide Diverse Students Multiple Ways to Demonstrate Learning

Use Formative Assessment To Identify Students' Readiness Levels   1 2 3 4
I use formal and informal formative assessment processes to identify my students' readiness levels.

Use Formative Assessment To Identify Students' Learning Preferences   1 2 3 4
I use formal and informal formative assessment processes to identify my students' approaches to learning in terms of intelligence preferences, learning styles, gender, and culture.

continued on next page

Learn Students' Interests   1 2 3 4
I use multiple processes to discover interests that individuals
and clusters of students have.

Provide for Student Learning at Diverse Readiness Levels 1 2 3 4
I group students in a variety of flexible groups to provide
instruction on essential concepts and skills at their level
of readiness.

Provide for Student Learning at Diverse Readiness Levels 1 2 3 4
I design differentiated learning tasks that are organized around
a common concept or skill that students can complete at their
level of development.

**Provide Learning that Accounts for Diverse
Learning Profiles**   1 2 3 4
I engage students in a variety of ways that give them
experience in different learning styles and intelligence
preferences.

Provide Learning that Taps into Culture and Gender   1 2 3 4
I design learning experiences that access the power of
and build on students' cultures and gender.

**Provide Students with a Variety of Choices to
Demonstrate Learning**   1 2 3 4
I regularly provide students with a variety of options from
which they can choose to demonstrate new concepts and
skills they've learned, including RAFT, TIC TAC TOE,
Learning Menu, and so forth.

**Hold Students to High Standards in Terms of
Curriculum Standards**   1 2 3 4
I design instruction and learning experiences that help all
students master essential concepts and skills from the approved
curriculum standards at grade level or above.

**Teach Students Basic Cognitive Skills as well as Study
Skills that Support Choice**   1 2 3 4
I systematically prepare students to exercise choice in how
they practice and demonstrate new learning, including basic
study skills, higher cognitive thinking and reasoning skills,
depth of complexity, and so forth.

Tools can be devices like hammers and chisels, or they can be concepts or strategies like deductive reasoning or chess moves. In the hands of inquisitive learners, tools can lead to innovation and change.

Dr. Shirley Jackson used tools at her disposal to create new technologies that led to inventions like solar cells, fiber-optic cables, touchtone telephones, portable faxes and more.

Calculators began as simple gears arranged by 17th century Blaine Pascal in order to help his father collect and compute taxes.

Everybody knows that Benjamin Franklin used a kite to discover electricity.

CHAPTER
NINE

Use Tools That Engage Learners

media ... manipulatives ... other resources

It was in a team meeting that Gil Kelton used the word "gamification" to make a point. "Games excite kids' minds," he said. "Principles of game playing give kids joy. When they face a challenge that piques their interests, they focus, they stay focused, they work harder. They chase a reward. If I can insert my goals for them into that experience, I'm ..." he paused for effect, "ahead of the game." The group giggled. "I've come to view gamification as an effective learning tool." He told the group about books he had read on the subject. [1, 3]

Clay added, "The power of gamification is that it offers a challenge. Facing a challenge gets your curiosity up. Overcoming a challenge, the process of trying to overcome a challenge—that's what gets your adrenaline going. You can just feel a reward around the corner, the reward of success."

"Even if it's not a game in the traditional sense?" Mary Pat asked.

"Especially if it's not a traditional game," Marge interjected. "I don't have time for games just for the fun of it."

"Gil, I liked your words 'principles of game playing,'" Mary Pat said. "I don't use many traditional, off-the-shelf games in my classroom, but I get what you and Clay are saying. When we give some kind of challenge to students, we engage them."

Incorporate Elements of Gamification into Learning

Mary Pat's group offered ideas they've used to gamify some of their lessons to increase student engagement.

"Sometimes when we are working on a word problem, I break it into steps and give kids a time limit for each step. I project a stop watch onto my screen so they can see how much time they have left for each step. It is a simple rule—get this step done in 90 seconds—but it's a useful challenge because each of them wants to be the first to get it right," Mary Pat said.

"I put props right into their hands, like dry erase boards," Marge added. "I make them compete against each other to be first to show me the right answer."

"Have you tried leader boards?" Dan asked. "I've heard they work well in the same way—to increase competition between students or between groups."

"Achievement boards do that, as well," Gill said. "They record which students have completed certain tasks. You can apply it to any projects or tasks like steps completed in a project or mastery of a series of skills.

"What engages learners is a direct point of connection such as the challenge in a game, the sharing of discovery or progress with classmates, or the potential for reward that a device can offer."

"Manipulatives," Marge said referring to the physical, visual, or digital objects that teachers often use to model concepts, ideas, or systems. "The right objects are useful for creating a hands-on learning environment as they engage students in visual and kinesthetic learning."

"Manipulatives are used often in a constructivist approach to discovery learning," Gil added, "in which students are free to interact with an object, the manipulative, and to gain knowledge through the interaction."

Naturally, the type of manipulative must suit the topic to be learned as well as the age of the students.

"I constantly search online for ideas about manipulatives," Mary Pat said. "When I student-taught at an elementary school, I used multi-colored unifix cubes for sorting and pattern activities. The colors and sizes make them easy to count and sort which makes them very useful for learning the basic math facts and discovering the properties of the different operations.

"I had students put the first number in an expression in one color and the second in a different color and then gave them problems such as 5+3 and 3+5 so they could discover the commutative property of addition for themselves and be able to describe it for themselves."

Marge added, "And some variations on Unifix cubes like fraction cubes help students see and interact with fractions. Fractions themselves are abstract so cubes make the abstract idea concrete, and I add labels to help link their interactions with the writing conventions. And I've used coins and chips to represent positive and negative."

"Me, too," Mary Pat said. "And algebra tiles are the next step in their mathematical progression. They can now express not just fractions and whole numbers but any number in the form of variables. When combined with an equation mat or an expression comparison mat, the tiles can make the abstract ideas of algebra something concrete because they can be manipulated by hand."

"And you don't have to spend a lot of money buying algebra cubes or tiles," Marge added as the bell rang. "You can print out some of your own and just laminate them!"

Consider Manipulatives and More

Every step in every instructional plan holds the potential for tangible interactions between students and a specific concept or skill you want them to master. The world of physical, visual, and virtual manipulatives seems endless, so the challenge for you is to search for and match the right manipulatives with your instructional goals, your learning outcomes. Here are some categories to consider in your search:

Models engage students in hands-on learning. A physical demonstration model like an atom, a globe, or a solar system allows students to manipulate and work with objects—to see them, to touch them—in ways that would otherwise be impossible. A model brings unreachable qualities into the hands of each student. For instance, you can make geometric dimensions or relative distances make more sense to students because the interactional experience brings the concept into their immediate world. Often, English teachers find models of things students are reading about such as maps or models of buildings or ships. Science teachers have directed students to handle simple machines in order to understand certain principles of physics. History teachers sometimes engage students with battle diagrams or topographical models to think more deeply about an event, or they have students interact with thematic charts that reveal demographic or sociological information.

Measurement tools help to build numeracy and a sense of scale. And such tools do not always have to be rulers or scales. You can use thermometers, anemometers, measuring cups and more to have students quantify aspects of a situation or condition in order to gain deeper understanding.

Dice and coins are handy manipulatives, especially for sparking interest about a concept or skill in the context of a game. The very randomness of this kind of manipulative sparks interest and keeps an activity fresh.

Story cubes can be building blocks of content and context. Some teachers simply glue words onto blocks to have students build sentences or parse the syntax of sentences. Story cubes can ignite student imagination and creativity, they are great tools for collaborative tasks, and they easily serve as vehicles for information that you want students to collect, sort, organize, and otherwise manipulate in the context of the goal, the learning outcome, that you have planned.

Virtual manipulatives show things three-dimensionally, which can be very exciting to students. The internet offers a wealth of virtual models. For instance, *Google Earth* enables virtual tours of locations, assists with measuring distances or looking at mountains and buildings, gives students access to measure the world and its mountains, cities and valleys—possibilities just keep coming. Students can see the weather in real time while focusing on global issues like water sanitation or animal conservation. Another one, *Solar Walk*, helps students watch how the Galaxy is spinning in real time. They can speed up, slow down, or go back in time; they can zoom in to see individual planets and moons. Math teachers can plan for students to manipulate virtual balance scales on screen to solve equations. History teachers can take students on virtual tours of historic sites. An added benefit: when you are using a virtual manipulative, you have no mess to clean up afterwards.

Use Tools of Technology To Enhance Instruction

Resources online and at hand can be your teaching partners by providing information, support, and opportunities—some of which weren't available until only recently while some will be available tomorrow or the day after! Think of an instructional tool as your own personal assistant or teacher's aide.

In all its forms and with all of the wonders it can access, technological resources open doors for us—at home, at work, in school. Everyone now knows that the computer makes editing and revising so much more effective than a typewriter once did. A calculator enables many complex operations that would be complicated to perform on a slide rule. Equally exciting is this: as technology advances, so do our chances to improve how we do things, including how we teach and how students learn.

Consider How To Redefine Your Instruction

Understand the potential for enhancing instruction and for engaging students interactively through various media available to you. But be sure to build your knowledge base by accessing the information on these pages and by consulting with your technology specialist(s) in your school, who probably have deep interest in—and knowledge of—the readiest tools. In fact, your technology leader may find your work on a lesson plan rather exciting and will be eager to suggest ways to augment, modify, and redefine the actions you are planning. Here are some examples of ways teachers have redefined their instructional plans:

A teacher decides to "flip the classroom" by assigning a presentation for students to view and/or interact with at home, followed by subsequent in-class focus on related activities, practice, and interactions with each other and the teacher. The "flip" is the use of technology at home to do the initial direct instruction or to provide the initial experience. Class time, then, focuses on expansion and application.

Or students watch a teacher's videos at home and take notes while simultaneously answering formative assessment questions on their computers. The next day in class, the teacher has learned via computer which students struggled with the concept and is thereby able to focus more on working with students and less on presenting.

In another class, students may be working collaboratively on a presentation using something like *Google Slides*. All students can see each other's progress, they can edit in school or at home, and they can insert images, links, and videos. They share their presentations simultaneously and in real time, thus saving class time that would have been spent watching each presentation one at a time.

Always as you learn about new and various tools and products available, think about how these can help you transform the way you present information and engage students.

Make Use of Computers and Projectors

Surely, you already have used technology in your classroom, and you will continue to do so. Technology continues to develop and change—everybody knows that—but what also develops are new ways of using existing technology.

Arguably the most familiar and easily available teacher "aides" are computers and projectors which can add vital, real-time experiences for students. If you can add a projection screen to a classroom computer, you have the ability to engage each student no matter where s/he is located in your room—watching from a desk, engaged in group work at a table, working with a partner at a station or carrel. Such technology ensures that each of your students has a front row seat to an important learning experience. Consider the difference between a teacher describing the process through which a cell divides while drawing an image of the cell on the whiteboard versus a teacher who shows a video to the class of actual cells dividing. How much more meaningful would your students find the words in the U. S. Declaration of Independence if they could simultaneously see a painting of the Boston Massacre or Boston Tea Party, a gathering of the First Continental Congress, or a video clip from *1776* or *Johnny Tremain*?

Make a habit of adding this question to your lesson planning: *What images can I add that will provide context, create interest, or demonstrate something for my students?* Find and embed these images into your lesson plan.[1]

How and where can you find such images? Many teachers begin their hunt with an internet search using an engine like *Google* or *KidzSearch*. Some use *YouTube* or other social media outlets.

As you locate images—pictures, graphs, video clips, etc.—that you wish to use, keep in mind some important aspects:

1. Make sure you are not infringing on someone's copyright of the material. This is fairly easy to do by clicking on a link like "search tools" and then look for additional links to such things as "usage rights" or "license" or "not filtered by license."

2. Once you think an image appropriate for your lesson, look for an option to "copy image" and do so by clicking. See if you can paste it directly into your lesson plan document or other location like *Power Point* slides that you plan to use.

3. Another way to display the image is to right-click on it and then to select "open in new tab."

4. If you want to embed the image in something like *PowerPoint*, right click the image and then select copy

image. You may see something called "Paste Options" in your document which offers you additional choices for adding and formatting your image.

5. WARNING: As you or your students search for images, inappropriate material may pop up. To prevent this kind of intrusion, look for "safe search" settings that enable you to filter inappropriate material. Another approach is to rely on kid-safe search engines like *KidzSearch*.

Expand Learning Experiences with Computers and Projectors

You know this already: most kids love (and "get") technology. Your classroom projector can improve students' presentations as much as it can improve your own, but first your students need the necessary tools at their disposal (and yours). If you think it will help—and it may with very young students—schedule a brief talk by your school's technology person or other colleague knowledgeable about presentation programs. If that person is YOU, then help students become adept at using products like *PowerPoint*, *Google Slides*, *Pages*, *Microsoft Office*, and others.

Pointers like the following may help orient students to the products and procedures involved in selecting and uploading images into presentation software.

1. Determine and describe key differences among the various presentation products you have available for student use.

2. Most programs have image search functions within their navigation tools. Help students recognize where they are and what they do. This may be an opportune time to explain copyright infringement and the various tools within products like *Power-Point* and *Microsoft Office* that help filter out proprietary images (material that its owners haven't permitted for commercial or public use).

3. If you expect students to display their work on your projection screen, explain how they can email theirs

(e.g., to your classroom computer) as an attachment or how they can save theirs on a flash drive for you to upload. Suggest that they save their documents to online storage or sharing programs such as *Google Drive* (or *Drop-Box* or *OneDrive*) which will allow them easy access.

4. Students may find some products complex—*Power-Point*, for instance—so it may be helpful for you or a techno-helper to hold a session to review the various formatting options. Ideally, you can do this in a way where students can practice using these options during such a session.

5. Many students have success with *Google Slides* because they find it easy to use. Also, it's free and available to students wherever they have internet access—in school or at home or elsewhere. Each student can establish his or her own *Google Drive* account and can work within that account at will.

Technology aside, certain classroom management strategies have a place in your 21st century classroom:

1. Set clear expectations. Let students know how you will evaluate their work products. If you think it will reinforce student learning about their technology options, include aspects in the evaluation such as *How Well Images Support the Topic, Appropriateness of Images Choice, Incorporation of Multi-Media into Presentation*, etc. You can make your technology expectations specific by identifying *audio, images, video*, and *hyperlinks* as specific aspects of technology.

   Help students avoid technology clutter; help them understand that too many multimedia aspects (e.g., over-loading a presentation with videos and images) can detract from the central message. Let students know that you will evaluate on conciseness, so students can select the most useful multimedia aspects.

2. <u>Manage time and set time limits.</u> A due date is obvious—all students want to know that piece of information—but you can help students manage their time if you give them time limits for *the steps within* their work as they develop their presentations.

3. <u>Use management techniques like cueing and proximity.</u> Students will work independently or in pairs or groups. As they accomplish things like locating images, uploading them, re-formatting them, and merging them into presentation software, draw attention to their successes (for others to learn from) or to their struggles (to enlist others in finding solutions) or to their questions (which other students may not yet have answered for themselves). This kind of cueing enables increased understanding and maximizes success and creativity. Your use of proximity (movement around the classroom) will increase your chances for mining golden opportunities for growth.

Consider Using a Document Camera

A *document camera*—sometimes called a *visual presenter* by hardware suppliers—has a high-resolution lens that can zoom and photograph very small things as well as three-dimensional objects and can project those for all to see. One advantage of a document camera is its storage capability so that you don't have to carry the document or item to class, just the camera or a file that you up-load into the camera. With most models, you can project from the camera directly, or you can attach the camera to your classroom computer or to networked computers in your classroom. A commonplace use of document cameras is for displaying examples of student work, works in progress, common mistakes and revision techniques, but the list of possibilities is practically endless.

Connected to a computer, a document camera doubles as a webcam, thus enabling a variety of uses. You or your students might create videos. You might record yourself solving a math problem on paper while projecting each of your steps to the class or to a group. Many document cameras work with Skype for others to participate in a lesson with you.

Many teachers have searched for education technology solutions and have found applications that expand the capabilities of a document camera. One example is a vendor like *MasteryConnect* that can turn the document camera into a grading tool. Using their software, you can use your document camera to grade multiple choice tests or surveys instantly. You can have students hand in multiple-choice formative or summative assessments and have results immediately. Technology like this enables you to take practical and intellectual leaps that you could not have done previously with simple paper and pencil, black or white boards.

> **Note to Self:** Projecting something *interactive* allows new ways for students to learn.

One-to-One Devices Can Transform Learning

When each of your students has a web-enabled device, you have enormous opportunities for individualizing your instruction and your students' explorations, all of which leads to heightened learning. In your lesson planning, where you have identified topics that students can explore as part of their independent research or as their contributions to group work or work in pairs, be sure to focus the tasks ahead of them so that they can get started actively.

Guide Your Students' Online Research

For instance, give students suggestions about various media (text, video, charts and graphs) that may best suit the task ahead of them. Review online sources by name, such as *Wikipedia* or *KidzSearch Encyclopedia* or *Google Scholar.* Make a list of keywords (search terms) that students might use in their searches. If you think it will make a difference or help students focus their team efforts, suggest different search terms for different groups or for specific tasks within group work.

Point out that url endings like *gov, edu,* and *org* will differ in the kinds of information students will find there. Tell students that they can go to the advanced settings in a search engine to select *.gov, .edu,* and *.org* for the domains.

> **Note to Self:** Keeping a growing list of helpful web pages increases my resources for future planning. Have students evaluate each web page for its helpfulness.

If students are using their devices to gather information to use in a presentation, focus their citation skills. Help them to cite their electronic sources in their presentations.

Guide students during their research process online. Specifically, help your students think critically as they delve deeper. Teach them to ask questions like these:

1. Is this information current? (Tell students to look for dates that indicate when the page was last updated.)

2. Is this information from a trusted source? (Find the author of the material and his credentials. If students cannot find an author or credentials, tell them that they should be skeptical about the validity of the information.)

3. Is the author or organization that made the website biased? Does the author or organization appear to seek compensation or future business? (Use your judgment in guiding students about the objectivity of authors and organizations they come across.)

4. Does this website seek personal information? (Advise students not to offer personal information.)

5. Does this website cause pop-ups about viruses? (Advise students to close such a site.)

If necessary, give students practice researching a topic along with you, especially if you think some students have greater facility than others with one-to-one devices. Give students a topic they all can comprehend. Follow these steps:

1. Discover Online Resources: Start this activity by giving students the task of finding one or two good web resources on the topic: a link or two. Tell them to paste the link into a *padlet* (padlet.com) that you have created for this activity. (Note: A padlet is an easily-created website where students can leave small links or comments. It is like putting sticky notes on a large poster.) And remind each student (a) to enter his or her name in the padlet, (b) to enter the link, and (c) to type a brief paragraph summarizing the content, the purpose, and/or other aspects of the website.

2. <u>Compare Resources:</u> Ask students to share the resources they find. If you can project for all to see, discuss the apparent benefits of those links.

3. <u>Evaluate Resources:</u> If you open some of the links for all to view, ask students to think critically about each one to determine which best suits the topic.

4. <u>Manage Time:</u> Be sure to give students clear time limits for each leg of this activity.

Help Students Expand their Research Options

Consider the vast array of resources available. Think about ways you can incorporate the following kinds of resources:

1. A **virtual manipulative** is an interactive program that allows students to manipulate an image and see the results of their changes. Here is an example of a virtual manipulative on the *GeoGebra* website created by Roy Wright.[6]

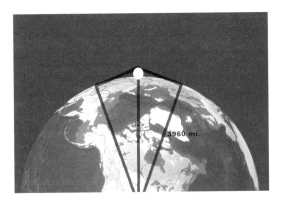

In this manipulative, students can move the dot higher or lower, thus making the height and arc length change instantly along with the rest of the illustrations.

2. A **productivity app** is an application that allows students to perform functions like calculating, drawing,

sharing documents, adding audio into a presentation, and so many more. Google, for instance, offers a wide range of productivity apps like *Google Docs*, *Google Sheets*, *Google Slides*, *Google Forms*, and *Google Drawings*.

For students, these can be especially useful as they work on independent projects or on group tasks. For instance, multiple people can have a document open and all can work on it simultaneously.

For teachers (and others), *Kaizena* is a *Google Doc* add-on that allows you to leave audio feedback for your students by highlighting the text to focus on so you can record your voice for students to listen to later.

3. A **collaboration tool** or an **add-on** enables students to work together or with you. *Kaizena* is an add-on that allows for audio feedback through *Google Docs*. *Google* offers many different kinds of add-ons. In *google.com*, for instance, you can open a *Doc*, *Form*, *Sheet*, *Drawing*, or *Slide*. When you enter any site offering these kinds of resources, look for key words (*Math*, *English*, *Geography*, *Art*, etc.) to explore related add-ons.

In *Slides*, for instance, each student can work on an individual part of a presentation while others work on their parts. In *Docs* students can write, edit, and revise writing with peers or the teacher. In *Drawings*, students can work collaboratively to create an attractive image complete with text, hyperlinks, drawn images, and copied images. In *Sheets*, students can evaluate a collection of data and can manipulate that data. And students can use *Forms* to create surveys that they can share.

4. A **HyperDoc** is a digital lesson available through one of *Google's* productivity apps. Imagine this: you create a lesson plan or agenda in a *Google Doc* and then share it electronically with each of your students. The lesson opens with an attention-getting prompt. Students respond to the prompt within the document or by

clicking a link in the document to go to a Google form. Naturally, you hold each student accountable for answering the question, and all students are able to read each other's comments. Then you follow the starter with a presentation that you can link to a video for them to observe followed by a task to perform. You might even add a worksheet via link in the HyperDoc so that each student can copy it to his or her drive to work on it. And then your lesson ends with a formative assessment in *Google Forms* or some other app.

As your students work—at their own individual paces, of course—during all phases, you can observe and interact with each while differentiating their learning.

And there is so much more that you can do using Hyper-Doc. You can use this technology to help you create a learning environment in which each student progresses at a pace that works for him or her. You can share learning modules to keep parents involved with their children's homework and their progress as well as your curricular expectations, and you can help students keep up if they are ill or otherwise homebound for a period of time. [2]

Assess Your Students' Online Research

Online you can find sites to help you assess student progress formatively, quickly, and efficiently. *Flubaroo*, to name one, turns *Google Forms* into automatically graded assessments. Here are more formative assessment programs and apps:

1. **Kahoot.it** contains—and helps you create—multiple-choice assessments that students find engaging. Generally, these work through the projection apparatus of a teacher's computer.

2. **Socrative.com** provides options for multiple choice, short answer, and true/false. It even offers quick question options so that you can create a new or additional question in real time. There is even an option for the students to vote for their favorite response, which takes *think-pair-share* to a new level.

3. **EdPuzzle.com** integrates with *YouTube* to create videos with assessments incorporated. It works this way: you select a *YouTube* video (or any of the many educational videos already available) and then use the *EdPuzzle* interface to insert short answer or multiple choice questions at specific points in the video. Students cannot continue through the video until they have answered the question or listened to your commentary. In addition, *EdPuzzle* enables you to create videos with formative assessments as homework, which allows you to determine how well each has understood the presentation. By the time class begins, you can be ready to help the students who most need it while providing extension activities to those who understand it really well.

4. **Edmodo** is a very large online resource that helps you organize lessons and assignments by handing out assignments, assigning and grading quizzes, sending students digital resources, creating class calendars, contacting students individually, and more. The quiz feature allows you to create multiple choice, short answer, fill in the blank, and matching questions.

5. **Nearpod** is a classroom presentation resource that converts *PowerPoint* presentations into formative assessments and interactive lessons with engaging aspects. For instance, it has a polling feature that uses a multiple-choice question format to collect, tabulate, and display students' responses in pie chart form. Its Drawing feature allows students to draw on an image in order to respond to a question. Its open-ended activities allow students to write their own responses to a question which they can share individually with the class. And there is a quiz activity that allows you to create multiple-choice quizzes that will be automatically graded for you.

Consider More Options

Technology offerings change frequently so it makes sense to search continually for the types of apps, tools, and other applications that expand learning possibilities within your classroom environment. Here are a few more:

1. **Student Response Systems, or clickers,** are small devices that look like remote control devices. They come with a variety of response options depending on the specific brand and model that you choose. While students use these to respond to questions, you can receive a tally—a histogram—of their responses so that you can determine immediately how well students have understood.

   A clear benefit of using clickers is that you can ensure that every student responds, not just the ones who normally raise their hands. And some clickers offer you various features that increase student engagement.

   You can use clickers for instant grading of assessments, thus saving you precious time.

2. **Drill programs** provide repetition for practicing a specific skill, and some provide instant feedback to students as they use it. Many current reading and math drill programs have students practice spelling, reading, and calculation skills by repeating the same type of problem, but research suggests you should use these sparingly and in special circumstances where repetition fills a specific need.

3. **Tutorial programs** provide instruction in a variety of ways from simple direct instruction to interactive videos. Khan Academy is an example that provides lessons for all content areas.

4. **Game programs** provide opportunities for students to engage with learning through games. Be aware that while many of these appear highly motivating, many take the form of simple drills, which do not help with higher order thinking. Look for problem-solving, but be aware that more complex games are harder to find, especially when you are looking to match it to a specific objective. Search carefully.

5. **Simulation programs** provide virtual space to simulate real world actions and objects. For instance, they can simulate lab experiments when supplies are short, or they can simulate how gravity interacts with multiple planets of differing sizes.

Keep in mind that you can find still more programs to assist with special needs. *Google Translator* can help a teacher communicate with a student who has not yet learned English while helping that student learn a new language. Text to speech software helps students who struggle with reading. Speech to text software helps students who struggle with writing.

Let's Not Forget Cell Phones

Not every classroom comes well equipped for technology, but most students come equipped with it anyway: Cell Phones!

Most, if not all, of your students are able to connect to the web and web resources through their phones, and they can find most of the programs and apps you know about. Cell phones can be your clickers and computers. If not all students have cell phones, perhaps you can find just enough devices provided by the school to make up the difference.

However, be aware of certain pitfalls. Your students already have multiple social uses for their phones, so you must monitor their use during class work. One way is to instruct students to leave their phones in the top corner of their desks at all times. Have them turn phones face down when they are not in use for direct access to the work of the lesson.

Use Technology To Supply Interventions

Because so many technological resources exist for helping with interventions, you may need to search for these narrowly. Use precise keywords to identify the content area and the specific need. Here are some well-known sources:

1. **MobyMax.com** tests students for their current proficiency, it identifies gaps in proficiency, and it provides lessons and assessments to help the students move forward.

2. Some **online textbooks** come with online applications that help to guide students who are struggling
   with the homework. This may be in the form of
   providing a hint, showing a similar type problem
   (e.g., in math), offering videos, or guiding the student
   through the steps in finding an answer.

3. **Socrative** and other assessment programs can also
   help with interventions by using them for formative
   assessments. Programs like these help you to identify
   needs early in your instructional process so that you
   can provide additional interventions in a timely
   manner. You may even decide to continue working
   on a concept until you reach a goal of proficiency
   such as 80% of students scoring 70% and above. Such
   practices create a pacing that is in line with students'
   abilities.

Use Technology To Supply Extensions

Students who excel are ready for their next level of learning.
Technology helps reach those higher levels of learning by helping
such a student create a product, for instance, because this kind of
work encourages analysis, evaluation, and creativity. Technology
helps students synthesize the information they gather, and it allows
them to evaluate their work and the work of others.

Using *Google Slides*, for instance, students can create a very
basic presentation containing videos, images, and text and they
can go further by turning their slides into a video using *MoveNote*,
which integrates with *Google Slides*. Students can easily create videos using apps such as *Screencastify*, *YouTube*, and *PowToon*. All
of these products are available for free. As students create video
presentations, you are encouraging them to think about and engage
with the content on a new level.

ThinkLink is yet another way students can combine information by taking an image (or by creating one) and then by adding
links to different items in the picture. For instance, students might
use a map identifying battle sites during the U.S. Civil War and add
links at these locations to relevant websites, videos, or perhaps
even their own work from essays.

Consult Experts

1. Chou, Y. *Actionable Gamification: Beyond Points, Badges, and Leaderboard.* Fremont, CA: Octalysis Media, 2016.

2. Highfill, L., Hilton, K., and Landis, S. *The Hyper Doc Handbook: Digital Lesson Design Using Google Apps.* EdTechTeam.com/Press, 2016.

3. McGonigal, J. *Reality Is Broken: Why Games Make Us Better and How They Can Change the World.* New York: Penguin Books, 2011.

4. Moultin, J. *The Power of the Big Screen: The Digital Projector Makes Instructional Materials Larger Than Life.* http://www.edutopia.org/power-big-screen, July 18, 2006. online

5. Shrock, K. *SAMR and Blooms.* http://www.schrockguide.net/samr.html, 2016.

6. Wright, R. *How Far Can You See?* https://www.geogebra.org/m/MvcjQQek

Self-Assess: My Use of Tools To Engage Learning

For each element, self-assess using the following 1-4 scale:

1. **Missing (I need to do this)**
2. **Attempted (I try to do this, but I am not successful)**
3. **Apparent (I do this well, but I don't do it consistently. When I do it, it works!)**
4. **Well Done (I do this consistently and appropriately)**

Planning Engagement Strategies   1 2 3 4
I approach my lesson planning with an eye toward engaging students, where appropriate, with game-like or other motivational situations that challenge their senses of purpose as they strive to meet a specific learning outcome.

Incorporating Models and Manipulatives   1 2 3 4
I encourage a hands-on learning environment by incorporating models and manipulatives into students' learning experiences.

Using Technology for Presentations   1 2 3 4
I use hardware (projector, computer, doc cam, etc.) to demonstrate concepts and skills for my students.

Varying My Uses of Technology To Expand Presentations   1 2 3 4
I make regular use of presentation software (*PowerPoint*, *Slides*, *Nearpod*, etc.) and hardware (projector, computer, doc cam, etc.) to help students visualize or interact with new concepts and skills.

Using Technology To Enhance Student Practice   1 2 3 4
My students use technology as they work independently or collaboratively on objectives.

Using Technology To Enhance Assessment   1 2 3 4
I use technology for formative and/or summative assessments to grade faster, provide feedback, organize curriculum materials, track progress, or otherwise enhance the assessment process.

Using Technology To Enhance Communication   1 2 3 4
I make use of social media to better connect to students, parents, and the community.

Using Technology To Re-Vitalize Instruction   1 2 3 4
I use technology to create new and innovative learning experiences that engage students as they work in and outside the classroom.

My Level of Using Technology Overall   1 2 3 4
I estimate that my current level of technology use is 1, 2, 3, or 4.

Afterword

And the verdict is …

The end-of-year weeks revealed strange new feelings to Mary Pat. She dreaded saying goodbye to her students. Even with so much yet to accomplish before the last day of classes, she batted back a growing conflict between knowing that her students would move onward and upward to new things while knowing she would miss them and would not be privy to their next chapters—*well, not entirely*, she told herself, *at least I'll see them in the halls next year.*

Feeling just a little bit vulnerable, Mary Pat arrived for her end-of-year summative conference with Viola, who held open the door for her. They each took a chair at Viola's small round table next to the window. Mary Pat's students had boarded buses just 100 feet away. She watched as the silent yellow parade turned onto the service road and began to disappear.

Viola held a folder and an iPad, which reminded Mary Pat of classroom visits during the year when her principal entered observation data into that very same iPad with the bright green cover. "Let me show you my observation criteria," Viola had said back in October, a few days before her first classroom visit to Mary Pat's third period class, her most challenging. Viola had opened that iPad to her *ObserverTab* observation form which outlined the district standards and the specific performance indicators that she would be looking for. That initial meeting had comforted Mary Pat because the form described classroom management skills in such clear and concise terms that it enabled her to think in advance about how she would refine her teaching plans.

"This form gives me ideas for my planning," she had said to Viola during that meeting as the two examined the *ObserverTab* form together. "For instance, for indicator 2c (classroom procedures) you will be looking for aspects of time management during an activity, and the form tells you to listen for specific prompts related to starting and stopping. Well, that tells me I should script some prompts and post them!"

Viola had visited Mary Pat's classroom three times during the year, according to district requirements, and each time the two had met either prior to or after the visit. Mary Pat liked the pre-observation visits because discussing the forms gave her new ideas and helped her focus her planning. She liked the post-observation visits because Viola used the "reflective conversation" tools in *ObserverTab*, and these led to frank discussions about technique.

Now, near the end of Mary Pat's first year, she sat with her principal and wondered where this conversation would take her.

Viola began. "If I used only one word to sum up your year, Mary Pat—and I could find many words!—I'd use the word 'achievement.' I see achievement in your results with students, and I see real growth in your teaching practice." She watched as tears welled in Mary Pat's eyes. "You've been worried about this meeting, haven't you?" Viola answered her own question. "You needn't have, but that's something I see in most good teachers, the constant concern about getting it right."

Mary Pat nodded.

"That's what your plans and your performance have demonstrated to me: real achievement in measureable terms."

"Measureable?" Mary Pat glanced at the green iPad as Viola patted Mary Pat's artifacts folder. "Measureable," the principal repeated. "I see achievement in here." She opened the folder and removed one of the formative assessments that Mary Pat and her team had prepared and used early in the year. "I thought that you did a competent job designing questions that would reveal your students' ranges of preparedness, and you did a very thorough job of scoring their answers and identifying their different needs before you began your unit."

"I remember. I started by creating four groups so I could design different tasks for them. My early morning class is especially challenging. I have students working at the fourth grade levels and some at tenth grade."

"I like your word 'designed,' Mary Pat, because that is exactly what you did. You deftly designed well-tailored instructional pieces that you delivered as each of those four groups worked on those different tasks, which you also designed precisely to build the skills they were needful of. And you made it work by giving direct instruction to each group separately on those skills.

"What impressed me just as much, Mary Pat, is that you scheduled your planning time—your 'designing' time—and your in-class assessment time to give you enough time to design the interventions and extensions."

"Actually, I started designing the different group work—and the small group lessons that I planned to give to each group—as I wrote the formative assessment questions but, I admit, it was a bit of a sprint for me to scan the assessments, identify and group the students, and then refine my group plans. Over time, as I worked on CFAs [common formative assessments], I started to think of myself as a helpful, nurturing friend as I developed the interventions and like the leader of an expedition as I developed the extensions."

As Viola put away the pile of CFAs that Mary Pat and her team had devised over the year, she opened the green iPad. The screen lit up with one of the *ObserverTab* observation forms that Viola used for her classroom visits. "Back to my word 'achievement,'" she said. "I saw clear evidence of your students' improvement on tests ..." she paused, "and I checked. I recognized the potential effectiveness of your CFAs, so I wanted proof that they worked, and your students' grade improvements bore that out."

"I'm so relieved," Mary Pat smiled for the first time.

"And there is another way that I have measured your achievement." She spun the green iPad 180 degrees so that it faced Mary Pat across the table. "Do you see the portion of my observation tool labeled 'Student Engagement'?" Mary Pat nodded. "Well, every time I visited your early morning class, I entered the total number of students here," she pointed to the screen, "and I recorded the number of students actively, constructively engaged."

"That's why you circulated around my tables."

"Yes, indeed. Surely, I wanted to see exactly what students were doing and how their work varied group to group, and I recorded my verbatim observations. But also, once I enter class or group engagement numbers, *ObserverTab* gives me a specific percentage of student engagement."

"I remember. You showed me the form during our first meeting. The tool helped me understand your expectations."

"Yes, and over my visits during the year, the tool gave me a trend line of your students' engagement, and I'm happy to report that your trend line is UP. Considerably. Your student engagement rose from 62% in October to the benchmark of 80% by midyear and then to 90%."

Viola shared additional data from her observation forms. Mary Pat could see her personal achievement from a chart showing each drop-in visit over time. She could see achievement in her final summative score. However, Viola's "Depth of Knowledge" observation form indicated that Mary Pat still wasn't getting to the rigor she desired for her students, at least not consistently.

The two sat silently for a long moment. "I worked hard to implement each focus area that you brought to my attention and that Clay, my coach, assisted me with. I used to think that being a teacher was all about delivering content, but I had no idea how much of it is management, lesson design, and student engagement. I know I've grown this year. I'm proud of that. However …"

Viola asked, "What is one area you want to focus on as you plan for your next year?"

"Depth of Knowledge! Rigor. I know how to plan my lessons so they build concepts and skills properly, but I need practice leading my students to higher levels like DOK 3 and 4 [Depth of Knowledge strategic and extended thinking]. I worry that when state testing scores come back in, I will see some of my students didn't make the growth they could have due to my lack of experience in pushing them, in planning for rigor."

"Talk with Clay about this," Viola said. "Perhaps you can spend some time learning more about Depth of Knowledge and doing some pre-planning to increase the rigor in your plans."

Mary Pat agreed. The two discussed works by educators like Karin Hess and Norman Webb as well as online resources about strategies like "planning backwards" to develop rigor, and ways to scaffold sequences of questions and tasks for increased rigor.

Before she ended the conference, Viola asked Mary Pat to summarize her strengths. She put it this way, "What did you learn about your practice that you want to keep, to build on, and to incorporate next year?"

"From the first minute of the first day, I will focus on teaching habits. This year, I think I taught students what I expect, and I ask them to self-reflect a lot. I want to build on that because I'm good at it. I've been able to engage my students in self-assessing, in giving me useful feedback, and I think I'm learning how student engagement leads to their own achievement, so I want to get sharper at connecting their self-knowledge with the new concepts and skills in our lessons. I think I can expand my goals with rigor—depth of knowledge—by clarifying my expectations about rigor while involving my students in my planning."

"I'm excited for you, Mary Pat. You have had a most successful first year," Viola said. "And I'm excited for your students—this year, next year, and many more years."

"This means I'm keeping my teaching contract?"

"Now what do you think?" Viola rested her hands on her green i-Pad.

Designs for Planning Effective Instruction

9 Targets	Your Planning Focus	Planning Strategies (in brief)
1. Constituencies	Students Families Cultures Colleagues	• Celebrate cultural and personal differences. • Develop collaborative systems. • Tighten teacher-team functions.
2. Student Individual Needs	Learning Styles Student Profiles	• Differentiate through content, instructional process, and student product.
3. Curriculum Standards	Learning Objectives Learning Targets On-going Assessment	• Plan instruction from core standards. • Focus your learning objectives. • Articulate learning targets, and assess during instruction.
4. Formative Assessments	Vehicles for Pre- and Post-Assessment Interventions and Adjustments	• Create pre- and post- formative assessments. • Develop learning progressions. • Assemble and analyze assessment data. • Make on-going instructional adjustments.
5. Feedback	Two-Way Communication Delivery of Feedback Levels of Feedback	• Create and manage feedback clearly. • Target levels of feedback. • Use feedback to guide student self-assessment.
6. Content Area Knowledge	Language and Facts Subject Expertise Content Complexity	• Develop and share content of the discipline. • Use content language to challenge and engage. • Approach content in complex, rigorous ways.
7. Depth and Cognition	Real-World Connections Higher-Order Thinking Enhanced Cognition	• Discover real-world connections to curricula. • Help students manage diverse sources of information. • Plan extended projects that access real-world knowledge.
8. Differentiated Instruction	Diversity as Opportunity Choices Metacognition	• Explore and address learner differences. • Hold high expectations while providing opportunities for students to demonstrate learning in diverse ways. • Facilitate success through choices
9. Engagement by Devices	Media Manipulatives Other Resources	• Explore gamification in learning experiences. • Incorporate myriad opportunities—physical and technological devices—to expand communication and learning.